Streetwise Baltimore

The Stories Behind Baltimore Street Names

Carleton Jones

Bonus Books, Inc., Chicago

94 93 92   5 4 3 2

Library of Congress Catalog Card Number: 90-84624

International Standard Book Number: 0-929387-21-X

Bonus Books, Inc.
160 East Illinois Street
Chicago, Illinois 60611

First Edition

Printed in the United States of America

Contents

Contents

Acknowledgments

Scholarly studies of Baltimore's growth and its street pattern are, with one major exception, rather fragmentary. An early and entertaining article on the origin of street names appeared in the June, 1948 issue of the *Maryland Historical Magazine,* authored by the late Dr. Douglas Gordon, former president of St. John's College, Annapolis. Eleven years later, William B. Marye launched an elaborate series of commentaries in the same quarterly on city place names, more interesting to neighborhood buffs than street researchers, though the place and estate names often ended up on streets. For an in-depth portrait of where everything was in 1800, see "A Portrait of Baltimore in 1800," by Richard M. Bernard, also published by the historical magazine in its 1974 winter issue. The most complete study ever made of the city's physical growth is Sherry Olson's *Baltimore* (Johns Hopkins Press, 1980), a dense and highly elaborated chronology that is especially strong in showing the impact of manufacturing and port life on geography.

Most of these studies only touch incidentally on streets as a vibrant vector of urban life, a fun history. We must turn to journalists of the past half century for more lively and urbane treatments of the city's street story. Paramount among contributors—a pioneer, really—was Lee McCardell, foreign correspondent and long-time editor of the *Baltimore Evening Sun.* His account of the house numbering morass of 1888 (*Evening Sun,* April 17, 1940) is a classic example of enjoyable journalism tackling a ludicrous story.

By far the most extensive study of city street names and their history was performed by the *Baltimore Sun*

Magazine in a series dubbed "The Man in the Street." These were weekly articles, often illustrated with portraits of the men who got their names on the street signs, and written largely, but not wholly, by William Stump, then a *Baltimore Sun* staff member and later an editorial chief of the *Baltimore News American*. The series began in 1948 and continued without a break until 1954. The late Ralph Reppert and other local storytellers occasionally sat in. It is safe to say that this volume could not have done justice to the older streets of the city without using the Stump series as a research base.

A variety of sources provided the images in this book. I am specially indebted for counseling and locational help over a period of years to the library of the *Baltimore Sun*. Particular thanks are due chief librarian, Doris E. Carberry and staff members Carol A. Julian, Phyllis Kisner, Dorothy B. Lyon, Jean L. Packard, Yolanda A. Powell and Antoinette Scopinich. Other vital professional help has come from Mary Markey, supervisor of research inquiries for Baltimore's Peale Museum, a unit of the Baltimore City Life Museums and Paula Dozier, public relations coordinator for the Maryland Historical Society.

No book could have been completed without the willing expertise of the staff of the Maryland department of the venenerable Enoch Pratt Free Library, an unusual historic learning center within the city's public system. Thanks are due Anna Curry, director of the institution and Wesley Wilson, department director, and staff librarians Jeff Korman, Eva Slezak and Mary Catherine Kennedy.

I will close with thanks for help over a long time on visual images and their quirks provided by Frederick Rasmussen, photo librarian of the *Baltimore Sun;* Tom Beck, curator of photography for the University of Maryland Baltimore County and Dean Krimmel, research coordinator of the Baltimore City Life Museums. Readers and architectural and history buffs interested in pursuing physical treasures of city streets are referred to an unbeatable volume *A Guide to Baltimore Architecture* by James Dilts and John Dorsey, (Tidewater Press, 1981), the key to touring the city's surviving architectural heritage. For details on what is no longer there (thanks mainly to the organized urban vandalism of the 1950s and 1960s) see the author's *Lost Baltimore Landmarks*, (Maclay & Associates, 1982).

Court Square grandeur early in the century. The gaudy, towered post office was knocked down about 1930, and the lion rampant on the Emerson Hotel (at left) was hauled off to the landfill in the early 1970s. Today's North Calvert Street is one-way northbound with zero on-street parking.

Introduction

The streets of Baltimore . . . what a mixed image they present to the late-twentieth-century American. White marble steps stretching endlessly away into the horizon . . . battered and rusty factories at trainside . . . or grand harbor boulevards with flapping flags and radiantly lighted skylines at dusk.

Few who see the spectacle today realize that it has taken more than 250 years to shape it. When surveyors planked their rods into the ground, laying out city streets in the 1730s, they were inadvertently shaping the future. The basic outlines of their map survives today in the pattern of the city's downtown area.

In 1729, the Maryland general assembly authorized this laying out of a new port at the headwaters of the Patapsco River. New Orleans was already a generation old that year, and Virginians had been living on the land for about 120 years. But the assembly's action served notice, however dim, that the long dominance of the tobacco ports and commercial rule from Annapolis was waning. New roads were opening up the port to the products of the lush farmland of western Maryland and the Pennsylvania Dutch country. Showers of export grains were piling up, and the beginnings of mining were ahead. Baltimore, economically, was a natural act of creation, because it was close to so much that was new.

Legend relates that when it all started, only a single house, belonging to one John Flemming, stood on the original sixty-acre tract. The town was underway seventy years before the nation's capital was to be conceived forty miles to the southwest. Oddly enough, Flem-

Wagons of all sorts, including the western Conestogas, serviced the early city.

ming's house stood virtually on the corner of what is now ground zero of the city—the intersection of Baltimore and Light Street, just up from the present inner harbor.

Though it came relatively late into the brotherhood of colonial American ports, Baltimore, in its early street titles, paid homage to mother England and the power of the pound sterling. As the late Douglas H. Gordon, an international scholar and former president of St. John's College, Annapolis, once noted in the *Maryland Historical Magazine*,

> Names that precede the Revolutionary period are Cheapside, Fleet Street, Leadenhall Street, Lombard Street, Thames Street and Wapping Alley, all reminiscent of London. In the days before the mismanagement of the colonies by a party too long in power had brought odium upon everything royal, Hanover Street glorified the continental kingdom of the ruling family of England and Brunswick Street, Hanover's similarly ruled neighbor.

Despite this kowtowing to the all-important commercial umbilical cord to the mother country, the newly-planned town was far from a smash hit. Lots sold slowly. A half century after the founding of the town, a map shows an insignificant little place with a dozen or so built-up main streets, a diminutive harbor beginning only two blocks below Baltimore Street, and swampy land to the northeast on the Jones Falls borders that had to be crossed by a sort of causeway.

After its initial layout, Baltimore tried to extend itself much in the manner of Philadelphia to the north, with a neat street grid the basic pattern of planning. But in physical details Baltimore would more resemble hilly Boston. Philadelphia had dominated much of the business done in the core city in the early years. But town planners, such as they were, soon discovered that Baltimore could not ape William Penn's neat-looking plan for that "green country town" was built to take up all the flat space between two rivers.

In Baltimore, the block-by-block grid had to be tilted here and there at rakish angles to accommodate physical features, or halted altogether, moving sideways to go around obstacles, including the estates of wealthy landowners who refused to sell out and move. There were other physical hurdles. When Cathedral Street could not be extended southward, it remained a dead end, right in the middle of a thriving and prestigious neighborhood. Calvert Street for years featured one of the weirdest public facilities in the nation—a courthouse on earth berms, with a tunnel boring underneath it. For years, this freakish setup allowed merchants access to the northeastern side of the downtown business district.

The town site was shaped like a giant crab, with a ring of hills, then physically daunting in size, almost completely circling it at a distance of about eight to ten miles. Numerous waterways, major and minor, honeycombed the area—the north-south Jones Falls and the roaring, rambling Patapsco River to the west were the major players.

Though most of the street-naming of those early years has survived the centuries, the eighteenth-century town plot was not the first naming effort in the region. The Mount Royal area, which now serves as a center for art education, opera, and symphony, as well as serving as a home for Maryland state government departments, was originally surveyed in 1669. It was named Mount Royal by a Quaker miller from Pennsylvania; for what reason, it is not known.

Generally speaking, as the years passed, street naming was more important to the new town than estate titles, and in this process Baltimore was fiercely, almost naively patriotic. Anyone who acquired world fame (like Kossuth or Pulaski) by fighting for freedom got a street.

A remarkable quartet of names, perhaps unique in U.S. municipalities, reflects the city's desire to honor now-forgotten Englishmen who risked royal wrath by being on our side in the 1760s and 1770s when trouble was brewing. Two of them were tough old soldiers who knew the American Revolution was a hopeless cause, from the English point of view. Col. Isaac Barre and Field Marshal Henry Seymour Conway were the military men. Charles Pratt, Earl of Camden, rated two street names for his outspoken opposition to the king and commons. There may be still others lurking in the urban record somewhere. (For a fifth British-named street, see Chatham.)

Today Conway, Barre, Camden and Pratt streets are inner harbor fixtures. Barre has a historic restoration district named in its honor, Pratt is a highrise showcase, and Camden is a stadium site and an industrial park.

By the time of the revolution, street boundaries and property lines had become somewhat vague in many cases. The folklore of the times was exposed by property disputes, and could have influenced street patterns, for it settled land borders.

In 1786, attorneys were trying to settle the exact borders of a property called Cole's Harbor. They had to delve deep into the early eighteenth century, talking to old codgers who could remember way back. One day Miles Love testified that when he and John Ensor were sailing up the Jones Falls and had stopped at a landing, John had pointed out a rock, the boundary of the Cole's property. John had one better than that for the court. He said that when he was a kid he had chased a 'coon up a tree and wanted to cut it down to get the animal. But his father told him that the tree was another Cole boundary marker. Dad then said that people "could be hung" for chopping down a boundary tree. That made him remember. Tom Gorsuch backed up John's story about the tract and threw in one of his own. He'd once shot a wild goose from behind the same notable tree.

In a perhaps more important court deposition of 1786, one Jim Welsh helped out in a property case by identifying the exact spot where old John Flemming's house had stood. Welsh, then seventy-five, said he remembered the site of the Flemming house at the time when an agent for the Carroll family, who owned the site, had ordered Flemming off the land because "it was being surveyed for a town."

The stagnation and the primitivism of the colonial period would soon end. The peace of 1783 brought a new quickening into America's future, and the city was in a prime position to capitalize on it.

A Small City in a New Nation

Luckily for the immediate future, and as a fillip to expansion, Baltimore Street, when originally laid out, was eighty feet wide and ran straight through town for about three quarters of a mile. This yielded a far larger-than-colonial-era width, big enough to accommodate considerable variety in business ventures and in the size of wagons and coaches that could practically use it. The new route had the effect of tying major business down to the area west of the Jones Falls where it remains to this day.

The Three Loggerheads tavern, political headquarters of its waterfront district. By the 1940s, the city would have about 4,000 such watering holes.

East of the Jones Falls in the same post-revolutionary period was Jonestown, surveyed a few years after central Baltimore, scheduled to become one of the prime sites of Jewish pioneer immigration of the nation's history. Just to its north was Old Town, an area that grew more slowly than the center of town but which became the city's first theatrical district.

Lovely Lane, the founding church of American Methodism, in its courtyard off Light Street.

Fells Point, further to the northeast along the harbor, had the deepest water off its docks and could service heavier boats. Here the harbor's captains preferred to live, often over their stores and offices. Despite the point's advantages, Baltimore proper, by around 1800, already had about 150 warehouses, small and large, crowding 180 degrees of the harbor, brick structures that stored grain from the north and west and the processed grains from the thirty mills of the city. The inner harbor wharfage, just steps away from the counting houses of downtown streets, had by 1800 assumed a dominance it would maintain for many decades. Streets were built south of Pratt Street in the north harbor, out over the water on landfill bulkheads, to speed deliveries and unloading of imports. The merchants and the gentry lived surprisingly close to downtown in those days, at least in cooler months.

"Probably the most prestigious address in this

period was St. Paul's Lane between Baltimore (Street) and what is presently Saratoga Street," reported Richard M. Bernard in a 1974 survey of early Baltimore published in the *Maryland Historical Magazine*. The district would remain fairly intact until early in the twentieth century, when it was razed for the building of Preston Gardens. Lawyers found the area particularly attractive because of the nearness of the major courts. The area itself was known as the old "court" district. Members of the fraternity used to tell visitors that St. Paul Street, the main stem of their residential heaven, had been laid out by the cows, loping along the present path of St. Paul Place, down the Centre Street hill and up again to pasture in the eastern Mount Vernon area.

Severn T. Wallis was the acknowledged dean of the Maryland bar, and a landmark of the St. Paul Street "old court" district for half a century.

Various artisans and professionals other than lawyers also favored selected areas. Printers, food handlers, butchers, construction workers, tanners, and metal workers all chose different neighborhoods, near to their place of livelihood, as residences. As in many European centers today, including London and Paris, and unlike the present U. S. urban pattern, early Baltimore wealth lived downtown, while the poor took to the suburbs.

Oysters were eaten quivering fresh right off the boat on Patapsco and bay docks. The docks were streets themselves, with transient rooms and businesses.

The new expansion meant naming streets, and the original result was wide, deep, and predominantly male in cast. If women are honored in street names of the early years, it is by accident, or as a rare tribute from a husband developing a new tract of land.

William Stump, Baltimore journalist and editor, and one of the primary twentieth-century authorities on city street lore, has identified the post-War of 1812 period, the so-called "Era of Good Feeling," just before Andrew Jackson started stirring things up, as the source of the city's basic street-name pattern.

> Most of Baltimore's older streets were named in one great christening—some time between 1816 and 1822. It all started in the state's general assembly when that body, realizing that Baltimore was growing fast, determined to keep that growth orderly. To that end it established a commission made up of the city's prominent men, which it directed to draw up a map, complete with new streets that could serve as a master plan to be followed as the city grew.

John Eager Howard, the state's number one revolutionary hero, who had led troops well in both the northern and southern campaigns, was a member of that commission, along with eleven other worthies. It was not thought in the least out of order that most all the men on the original city planning board ended up with streets named after themselves.

The good city fathers even named streets after men who led the city survey, a remarkably warm gesture for a formal age. The men who had done the massive layouts of city ground plans were not forgotten. Hence both Jehu Bouldin, a local surveyor whose bid was too high for the post-War of 1812 mapping job, and Thomas Poppleton, the English surveyor who got the job, are both honored in street names.

By the 1830s, Baltimore had become America's third largest community. The physical size stretched beyond the abilities of coachmen, street vendors and ordinary natives to remember. City directories were underway, and the naming of neighborhoods as an aid to locals had begun. It was a complex process, and the bumpy nature of the terrain was a problem. Elevation irregularities shaped community names, as is obvious in the unusual number of areas that acquired the "mount"

Edgar Allan Poe, nineteenth-century poet and pioneer detective story writer, lived in this small, west Baltimore home in the 1830s. He wrote some of his best known short stories in one of its tiny bedrooms. The Amity Street house is now a museum.

designation. These names have survived, including Mt. Vernon, Mt. Royal, Mt. Winans, Mt. Washington, and Mt. Clare, giving a peculiarly English or Canadian tone to maps. Many non-mount names were also British, derived from the titles of the peerage and imbedded in neighborhood traditions, including Ashburton, Camden, Irvington, Fairfax, Fullerton, and Beaumont. There was also room for Italian (Montebello) and Irish (Dundalk) monikers for parts of town.

A sizeable number of neighborhoods became known by less pretentious titles, among them Federal Hill, Ellicott City, Lutherville, Catonsville, Cub Hill, Parkville, Putty Hill, etc. Chinese inspiration shows in the naming of Canton, the northeast harbor's long-active waterfront, not a "chinatown" (that is reserved for a short stretch of Park Avenue near the center city), but a district named in honor of Baltimore's link with the great Chinese port in the city's earliest days. Perhaps the bottom of the heap in neighborhood designations was Pigtown—a description of the ancient southwest industrial and blue collar region bordering downtown and inhabited by the animal its name honored.

When the city had run out of revolutionary heroes, English pals and city commissioners to name streets after, it could always fall back on destinations for inspiration. Baltimore is a "radial" city; not a complete circle

TOLL RATES

Forevery score of Sheep or Hogs.	6 Cents
Forevery score of Cattle.	12 Cents
Forevery Horse and Rider.	4 Cents
Forevery led or driven Horse, Mule, or Ass.	3 Cents
Forevery Sleigh, or Sled drawn by one horse or pair of Oxen.	3 Cents
Forevery Horse or pair of Oxen in addition.	3 Cents
Forevery Dearborn, Sulky, Chair, or Chaise with one horse.	6 Cents
Forevery Horse in addition.	5 Cents
Forevery Chariot, Coach, Cochee, Stage, Phaeton or Chaise with two Horses and four wheels.	12 Cents
Forevery Carriage of pleasure by whatever be it called, the same according to the number of wheels and horses drawing the same.	
Forevery Cart or wagon whose wheels do not exceed three inches in breadth, drawn by one horse or pair of oxen.	4 Cents
Forevery Cart or wagon whose wheels exceed three inches and does not exceed four inches in breadth for every horse or pair of oxen drawing the same.	4 Cents
Wheels exceeding four and not exceeding six inches.	3 Cents
Wheels exceeding six and not exceeding eight inches.	2 Cents
All Carts or Wagons whose wheels exceed eight inches in breadth. Free.	

DAVID T. SHRIVER, Supt.

You paid to get out of town in the old days (and into town, too) with various rates posted on tollhouse signs.

Wagons and buggies wait their turn at a westside toll station.

with an even radius, but more like a pie from which has been extracted a hefty slice in the form of the city's harbor. From the center of this pie radiate eight historic highways that, despite re-routings here and there throughout 250 years, have carried the freight of development. These are the York, Harford, Belair, Philadelphia, Liberty, Reisterstown, Frederick and Washington roads, each a "destination" title of clear meaning, each leading to a town or a city of essential moment to the city's early commerce and travel.

Two of these roads carry nationally-known and historic route titles, the Belair road (U.S. 1) and the Frederick road (U.S. 40 west). It is a point of some confusion that a few of these hoary routes have been chopped up into baffling little segments. Others have acquired the prefix "old," which doesn't help travelers. The most baffling example of this binary fission is the old Annapolis Boulevard (the Baltimore-Annapolis road), which has been chopped up into many segments as a grid of wider, faster roads has been laid over it. The result is that the boulevard leaps in and out of view and into dead ends with baffling inconsistency. Anyone who attempts to reach the Maryland capital from Baltimore over this route had better bring along a sextant and overnight gear.

Five miles from town on Washington Road, and you still turn only on the green arrow.

11

Baltimore growth has overlaid the old destination network, but it has not obliterated it. In fact, the giant freeway, Interstate 83, and the new Baltimore subway and its bordering Interstate 795 follow the historic routes of York Road and Reisterstown Road, respectively.

Such routes are living symbols of a much older city, of days when rapid growth helped determine the street and road pattern. The huge profits of city privateers who looted sea commerce at the turn of the eighteenth century helped feed a boom. In turn, this vastly increased the property values of the waterfront and the land near it. The record shows that the good churchmen of the First Baptist Congregation had to pay $10,000, a huge sum for the day, for their Lombard Street church lot 175 years ago. Lots simply became too expensive for any but the well-to-do to own. At the same time, with no public transport (and expensive sea or carriage travel only for the well-fixed), workmen had to live fairly close to jobs, almost all of which were situated around the harbor or up the mill roads of the Patapsco and the Jones Falls. A novel housing pattern emerged, one that for its day was progressive and shaped street patterns to a degree.

A harbor view of downtown on the 100th anniversary of the Revolution.

This system allowed both owners and workers to get around the huge cost of Baltimore city land. A "ground rent" system was developed and spread rapidly. The working man rented the land under his house for a small annual fee, or built on that land under a long term arrangement. In a typical situation, a family man would raise or borrow $400, for example. This money, often raised with the help of other men in the family or neighbors, was used to buy materials and hire help to put up a house. The land's owner would write a ground rent permitting tenantry of the land in perpetuity or for ninety-nine years as long as a fixed sum in interest, sometimes as low as $10 and rarely over $100, was paid annually. It got people into shelter fast. The system still exists across town today in a vestigial form, even though Maryland banks sold the rents wholesale to residents when U. S. interest rates began to soar in the late 1960s.

No stigma was attached to going the ground rent route, or not owning the land underneath your hearth, or, for that matter, in living in a row house. In fact, most of the town's famous full-time or part-time residents have gone for row house living—Edgar Allan Poe, John Wilkes Booth, Babe Ruth, H. L. Mencken, F. Scott Fitzgerald and a thousand others have been sheltered with wall to wall neighbors.

By the 1830s, low and moderate income families were universal occupants of rows. Street patterns (and the essential alleys for privies and outbuildings) had to conform to this modus vivendi in countless variations. By mid-century, even big mansion-type rows had ground rents, and they were often accompanied by an amenity alley nearby, which served as the homes of the help who tended the twenty-room rows, most often free blacks and Irish immigrants.

Another peculiarity of older Baltimore streets was the so-called "storage vaults." The competitive nature of the city's commercial heart put space at a premium. Building and business owners were allowed to tunnel under the streets and build cool, windowless vaults, particularly in the downtown financial district. Most often such space stored products and goods that were wholesaled or retailed above. One cloudy legend claims

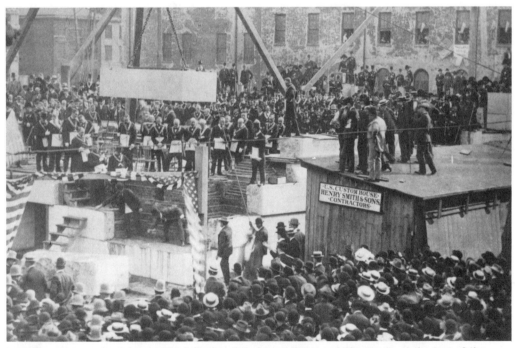

Launching a new customs house with full masonic honors at Water and Gay streets, at the turn of the century.

some of the vaults served as part of the underground railroad that smuggled blacks into the free territory of Pennsylvania. More likely, such vaults were used as temporary housing for slaves who accompanied southern planters on visits to the city's booming cotton market. Most of the vaults have been removed and are now illegal.

Baltimore plunged onward toward the tragic Civil War years; ever more polluted and, in the 1850s, engulfed in German immigrants fleeing the revolutions in the German principalities.

Once one has taken a realistic look at the city in the nineteenth century, one wonders how the residents got any sleep at all. The row homes faced on streets, but as late as 1899, cobblestones still comprised about 75 percent of the city's entire street pavement. Stanton Tiernan, a twentieth-century researcher, studied the street situation of the 1800s and 1900s and reported his results for *The Baltimore Sun* in 1940.

The awesome racket, the jolting rides, and the terrific podiatric and sacroiliac punishment endured by locals is unimaginable, but it must have been so general as to be taken for granted. Tiernan reported that these early street pavements were paid for by a lottery, plus a tax on carriages, sulkies, and even sedan chairs carried through the streets by flunkies of the lordly.

The cobblestones began as flat-topped granite blocks, but weather, water, and the shipping of metal wagon and carriage wheels wore them down into round patterns. "The stones acquired a rounded, polished surface on all sides, like true boulders," Tiernan says. When the lottery money was gone and the cash from carriages ran out, the city began selling hogs that roamed free in the public streets. "Finally, a two shilling six pence paving tax was put on every 100 pounds of assessed property within the town limits."

Tiernan's study could have noted that as awful as they were, the cobblestone streets of their day represented an advance over country roads. In the wet, winding country of central Maryland, the routes were often impassable for months. Rowboats and sailboats were the favored means of "getting there" in one piece. The coming of railroads actually worked to delay fixing the roads because no one dreamed of making long trips over local routes. In fact, Maryland did very little about country routes other than major turnpikes until well after the beginning of the twentieth century when it became almost overnight one of the first states to offer a uniform, paved system.

The Maryland shoulder—a widening and stabilizing feature for heavily travelled streets and roads, introduced by the Maryland State Roads Authority in 1914.

Still, the memory of those cobblestones lingers as a horror story. Paving was done by fifteen-man crews, including men who prepared the sand base and "chuckers" who carried the stones from the margins of streets to the pavers. The rocky result was particularly favored by dock and factory owners where heavy wagons would have chewed up a less durable surface. Sometimes the city fathers would try to pave with wooden blocks, but these became dangerously slippery when used on grades. The only sizable remnants of cobblestoning in the city, outside of a few dock area survivals, are portions of streets on or near Guilford Avenue in the north central city or historical restorations.

The Birth of Technology

Baltimore has always taken quickly to innovations in ground level transportation. In the 1830s it claimed the first regularly scheduled passenger service in world

A truck takes a dangerous shortcut around a traffic island, one of the city's first, at Pratt and Light streets. Manned islands with manual controls were the first efforts by harried traffic officials to regulate the flow of traffic.

history, starting at the Mount Clare Baltimore & Ohio railroad terminal and serving outlying Ellicott City. In the late 1850s, it began to revolutionize its street transportation system, which often consisted of glorified stagecoaches, old omnibuses that plodded from stop to stop. They were replaced with horsepowered "street railways." The change was universally applauded.

Rail power for the next eighty or so years was to become an indispensable tool of urban living, as well as the one essential for creating the suburban ideal, homes in more or less planned districts miles from job centers.

By the 1890s, when electric railways were booming, the efficiency of rail travel in metro areas was obvious. It is said that 500,000 visitors a day could be delivered to one place by existing trains, in this case, sightseers piling into Chicago's famed World Columbian Exposition, a volume that could hardly be reproduced in most urban areas today.

Workmen in one of the city's earliest auto shops are shown crafting one of the city's only ventures in automobile building—the Spoerer. Manufactured about 1914, it died after World War I.

The streets of the city required new engineering to accommodate the new locomotion system. One feature that survived into the 1950s was the peculiar "passenger island" that existed in scattered locations in the metro area and along York and Harford roads notably. These were marked street islands right on the blacktop where trolley customers would wait, right in the middle of fast-moving traffic streams. The little waiting areas were marked by pylons topped with blinking lights that were continually getting broken and being hit by cars. A community homily was born. It was said that a New Years Eve reveler, pedestrian, or driver who could get home safely over York Road was either very sober or had the right sort of saint on his side.

Another example of the city's willingness to go to any length to move people, using almost any and all methods, was the weird setup that survived a few years into the mid-twentieth century. Charles Street in central stretches of the Mount Vernon district near the downtown area allowed two-way auto traffic, plus both bus and streetcar service with parking on both sides of the street! And this on a street that had originated two centuries before and wasn't much wider than a sizable club cellar.

17

The celebrated street with two-way traffic, parking on both sides, and doubletracked streetcars—North Charles Street, urban nightmare No. 1.

Rail transit, both in the form of streetcars and "trackless trolleys" of the early twentieth century, was deeply imbedded in Baltimore's idea of urban amenities until it was given the coup de grace, with the sanction of City Hall, between 1945 and the early 1960s. Without the years of rail glory, the city would never have been able to develop either major industry or suburban life.

In the 1880s and 1890s, the vast growth of the city transit system on rails brought a new sort of street world into play.

High, healthy Catonsville was perhaps the leading sample of what street railway service could do for a community. This airy, western Baltimore county town, still more of a self-contained community than a mere commuter node in the metro web, got service of electrified cars over Frederick Road in 1895 and over Edmundson Avenue a few years later. A study in contrasts, cars of the Baltimore, Catonsville, and Ellicott City rail line sped past Mount de Sales Academy gate and Eden Terrace, a grandiose community of storied "Queen Anne" stone and shingle architecture, alive with jigsaw porches and weedy Victorian amenities of the potted plant age.

In the metro area, the heads of households rode such lines, returning to the sweltering city daily, while the family enjoyed country breezes. Workmen and mechanics to build and maids to service the huge mansions of the time could commute to job sites and were not tied to local employment.

It could never have happened, at least not on the scale that it did, had not the streets been engineered to offer alternatives to carriage and horsedrawn omnibus travel, at best expensive to maintain and uncertain as

You changed your own tire, even back in 1920. This photo of a man in a boater doing the honors at a vulcanizing shop proves it. The setting is Park Avenue hill.

transportation in violent or inclement weather. As a summering center, Catonsville became the wealthy German burgher heaven par excellence. With Boston and Philadelphia, Baltimore shared in the streetcar suburb mania of the turn of the century. But it wasn't all mania or dreams. By World War I, it was possible, with a few gaps filled in on conventional trains, to go from Baltimore to upper New England almost wholly on streetcars and light inter-urban lines, as preposterous as that sounds. (Admittedly, the route required an overnight stay about halfway there.)

Oldtimers who drone on about "the good old days" are almost gone from the American scene, but one of the good old things they really did have was an efficient, virtually pollution-free transportation system.

An event that can't go unnoticed, but perhaps meant less in the long run than one might think, roared through the city on a February weekend in 1904. The great fire of that year destroyed most of the city's central business district. About $200,000,000 in property vanished in 2,000-degree heat. Safes stuffed with millions in bonds and other securities plunged from top floors to basements and were allowed to cool for weeks before opening for fear of incinerating the contents with a rush of oxygen. But nobody died, at least that is the official verdict.

Oddly, the fire failed to change the city's structure. A few streets, including Light Street, were widened, the Pratt Street waterfront, completely incinerated for about a mile, was rebuilt with more solid structures, and what was left of the hoary, diseased old dock houses were torn down en masse on their piers. Little was changed, however. The rule was, rebuild in place to simplify the cleanup and the record keeping.

Vestiges of the old city lasted through the fire, even some of the street hardware. Three special cases were the town's hitching posts, carriage stones, and the "hokey carts." A few of the cast iron hitching posts have survived in place and are American collectibles. The carriage stones are also rare. These huge, square blocks were embedded in street pavement to guide carriage wheels up to the doorway of homes and establishments. They were equipped with stone steps embedded in the sidewalks, so that milady could dismount from her

20

The sweep of Pratt Street traffic at the peak of inner harbor dock prosperity, about 1935.

carriage without dragging her skirt through the mud. The hokeys were two-wheeled, man-powered street cleaners that survive today, even with more modern cleaning equipment in use.

A great personal trauma was inflicted on city residents, not the apparently endless rerouting of one-way streets in the 1950s (of which more, later), but in the summer and fall of 1888.

It was a sleepy, prosperous time in Victorian America, but suddenly all was not well in Mudville. Over the angry veto of the then mayor, James Hodges, the city council ordered a total renumbering of *all* the city's houses and commercial buildings—no exceptions. A bespectacled, brilliant busybody named T. Vernon Campbell started it all. Campbell (everybody called him "Bud") had founded a Canton area boiler factory. He took one look at the city's scrambled way of numbering homes and businesses and decided it was time for a

The Albion Hotel, a family place with separate entrances for ladies, basked in the mid-afternoon sun at Cathedral and Read streets, while summertime Baltimore napped.

change. Up to that time, the only system of numbering was based on the snaky path of the Jones Falls as it moved toward the harbor. Streets were numbered according to whether they were east or west of this benchmark. It was a weird division that ignored the fact that Baltimore men and women were scarcely authorities on whether they were east or west of the Falls at any given moment. Lee McCardell, legendary city editor of the *Baltimore Evening Sun*, sets the scene:

> Street numbers ran wild. Strangers went mad trying to follow them. The numbers didn't even follow a normal sequence. It was not unusual for a builder or a group of householders to arbitrarily designate a row of houses anywhere as a place, square or terrace. Such rows broke into established sequences with any old number that took their fancy and tapered off whenever the spirit moved them.

Campbell decided it had to stop. And he was well plugged in with most of the city's political bosses of the day. An ordinance was drafted, failed passage of the city council twice and then, to audible municipal groans, was finally put in force. The goal was to renumber the address of every single property in town. The corner of Baltimore and Charles streets, still the corner of corners in town, was selected as ground zero for the new numbering setup. Every address east or west of Charles would have to be renumbered. Likewise every single property north or south of Baltimore street. It was a daunting job, but Bud Campbell rode out the confusion and the storm, setting up a system where anybody could get their new number tacked up for twenty-five cents —four by two inch lettering in metal, some of which still survives on city buildings. If you bucked the system, you got a five dollar fine. If the two-bit numbers were not to your taste, you could install your own, more expensive model.

Nobody had the slightest idea how many homes and buildings would be involved. It must have numbered at least 80,000. Nevertheless, the revolutionary change was somehow carried out with widespread consistency, at least as far as the city's legal borders. The project also won the vast approval of sign painters and stationery companies who were offered extraordinary profits by the giant remake. For years, city directories

A vanished popular amenity; the movies, stores, and shops of West Lexington Street, an intimate, fun promenade buried under Charles Center redevelopment.

printed complex formulas for figuring out what an old number had been if you knew the new one (and vice versa). The most salutary effect was that Baltimoreans, who tend to be vague about directions, to put it mildly, were forced into a consistent and logical geography lesson. East was east and west was west and never the twain shall meet, except along Charles Street.

Naming the Streets in a New Century

With the death of local rail travel just after World War II, Baltimore, and most other U. S. metro areas, moved into the automobile age with a vengeance. Auto ownership and auto commuting doubled, then doubled again. Something had to be done, and in Baltimore, something was.

No other human power has had the modern-day effect on Baltimore's streets of Henry A. Barnes, the legendary traffic planner of the 1950s. He came on the scene at the middle of the century in order to straighten out what *Time* magazine called one of the nation's "most

23

The stagnant center city of the 1950s and 1960s. At this point, not a single large commercial office structure had been added since the crash of 1929.

gruesome" specimens of traffic congestion—Baltimore. It was a literal fact that in the 1950s, traffic sometimes took thirty minutes to move the fifteen or so blocks from Charles Street to the Johns Hopkins Hospital. A single viaduct carried jammed interstate traffic north and south between New York and Florida, with the result that Baltimore developed both a terrible urban reputation and a severe inferiority complex.

Though the community squealed in horror, Barnes took over this ugly stasis and began re-routing city streets. With airy aplomb, he took over the city's lighting system and its bus routes and the paths of John Q. Public as the poor soul tried to cope with metropolitan gridlock. The Bostonian narrowness of some of Baltimore's downtown street patterns complicated the job. And Mr. Barnes was no doubt told by Maryland's numerous amateur local historians that by 1889 congestion in the central business district had already become so general that wagons were banned in certain blocks.

Barnes did more than ban wagons; he revolutionized the downtown traffic system. The plan created a timed north-south one-way system that even today, with modifications, can send speeding motorists two or three miles in or out of town at thirty-five miles an hour. He was slightly less successful with east-west improvements, if only because the hills of the Mount Vernon district and the barrier of the Jones Falls valley combined to defy the building of logical routes that would not destroy whole neighborhoods.

As the Barnes revolution took hold, interesting things happened. At the intersection of Howard and Lexington streets, where four flourishing department stores once vied for tens of thousands of customers, Barnes created a four-way stop controlled by street lights for pedestrians. When the lights turned green, an ocean of people marched every which way, to four corners. The pedestrian miracle was immediately dubbed "The Barnes Dance."

In the Barnes years, locals would wake up one morning and find that next Tuesday their street was changing direction. The system took hold long after Barnes' departure for the *real* big time, the traffic system of New York City. Changes continued in a wholesale manner even after the chief left for the Big Apple. One 1970s traffic reversal, for instance, involved 2,000 new signs and 40 new traffic signals.

Lexington Street near the market house in the 1930s, a melange of vehicles turning every which way at will. Henry Barnes would organize things in coming decades.

In general, the business community supported the Barnes revolution. There were holdouts, however. Once, at a public hearing, a little old lady in lavender got up and said, "Did you know, Mr. Barnes, that Baltimore had the first gas streetlights in the world." "I certainly do," answered the chief. "I took one of them down last week," on the corner of so and so.

Though he was omnipotent when it came to stop signs and parking laws, Barnes did little or nothing to Baltimore street names.

Such restraint has hardly kept city council authorities from making changes for good reason, or even plausible whim. Occasionally, the city fathers would rise up in righteous anger and change the name of a street. One sample of this vengeance came one year when Republican Street suddenly was converted into Carrollton Avenue by the city's indelibly Democratic government. Far more famous a case occurred during World War I. German Street, a fixture of the downtown for at least five or six generations, became Redwood Street overnight, when the "Hunnish appellation of the Kaiser's Reich" proved too much to stomach. The City Council patriotically changed the name to Redwood, honoring Lt. George B. Redwood, the first Baltimore officer killed in World War I.

For a brief period the city tried European-style street signs stone-cut into buildings. Two cases where it didn't last were Republican Street at West Franklin (changed by Democrats to Carrollton) and Shirk Street at Charles. Poor Shirk apparently vanished under new building.

Occasionally, cooler heads would prevail in street-naming disputes. The practical would overrule the patriotic. The city turned down a request once to rename workaday Ashland Avenue (residents felt it sounded like some dump) to the name of a war hero said to have been "the first Bohemian-American" to die in the conflict of 1917–18.

Sometimes a name hassle would engulf a neighborhood, too. Sherwood was an idyllic country place on cool Baltimore county hills. Methodist ministers and their faithful had it changed to Riderwood (after a local family named Rider) because Sherwood was the name of a top-selling brand of rye whiskey.

On the whole, Baltimore has been patriotic and thankful in naming its streets, at least until the arrival of post-World War II suburbia, when a quite creative trend toward imaginative monikers took hold. But the town and environs has not been notably romantic about it all. Where are the memorials to the great beauties of the 1890s, Baltimore women so lovely their portraits were painted to order on the walls of a city university as the dying wish of a wealthy man? Where are the tributes to Lillian Russell, the Marilyn Monroe of the 1890s, or the opera queens of the golden age?

Handsome William Pinckney talked his way through seventy-one Supreme Court cases, but, like Tench Tilghman, goes unremembered in city street annals.

Washington aide Tench Tilghman brought the news of Yorktown to Philadelphia, but this Maryland "Paul Revere" seems unremembered in Baltimore's street names.

What about streets honoring the twentieth-century entertainment immortals who arose on city soil, names such as Eubie Blake, Blaze Starr, Billie Holiday and Cab Calloway? They do not exist, at least not yet.

Despite these ommisions, the list is rich. Virtually all the founding fathers and early presidents rate a street, sometimes many more than one, as is the case with Washington. A Timonium developer with a free hand and a sense of humor opened up a York Road section once near Padonia Road with tributes to Warren Harding, FDR, old George, and Abe. He then apparently ran out of names and filled in the rest of the tract with tributes to Rose, Thelma and Estella.

The record is mediocre in terms of delivering roads representing the fifty states, with only thirty-two represented. Most of the eighteen omissions are from New England, the Midwest and the Plains states. This is in line with the average Baltimore citizen's mastery of geography. The average Baltimore citizen seems to think mid-continental America is something you fly over to get to Las Vegas or southern California. Eastern and southern subdivisions of town, including Essex and Baltimore Highlands, feature the only major attempts to name streets—á la Washington, D.C.—after the republic's states. When the namers finally got wound up, however, they really did a number with Maryland and Virginia. They indulged in sheer overkill. There are about a dozen Maryland avenues and streets, and more than ten Virginias. None of the latter have the slightest thing to do with travelling south; of course, some may be tributes to wives or sweethearts, and not the old dominion.

The Essex-Baltimore Highlands' patriotic stance of naming streets for states resembles the efforts of the city fathers and surveyors of 1822 in dubbing dozens of inner-city streets in honor of War of 1812 heroes, the town's defenders in the years of the "Star Spangled Banner." The city went on to honor Mexican War standouts like Winfield Scott when the time came. But a veil descended with the Civil War years, and the town's mixed record in that conflict seemed to soft-pedal street memorials to officers.

The lackluster record of Maryland's Union army probably contributed to the lack of interest in creating street name memorials. The record with Confederates is curious. Rebel families like the Winders, Symingtons and Slingluffs have all achieved street name status, while nothing has been named for the Baltimore rebel to end all rebels, Gen. I.R. Trimble, a C.S.A. fire-eater. It didn't help when a family fought on both sides. The famed Shriver family of Maryland was split evenly for north and south but lacks a memorial, even in their native Carroll county. Confederate leaders like Lloyd Tilghman and Harry Gilmor have also not attracted a street sponsor.

By the Spanish-American and World War I periods, street-naming as a military honor was back in style, giving us Schley and Sims avenues, Redwood Street, and a few others.

A strong and visible preponderance of German names is much in evidence in street names christened from the 1880s through the 1920s, proof of the pre-eminence of German business men in the affairs of that era. Less stodgy methods and subjects were ahead, however, when the curtain went down on World War II and housing geared up.

Once Baltimore broke out of its traditional borders into open country, street-naming became less of a civic accolade for heroes and notorieties, and more a happy game of developers honoring wives, and occasional girl-friends, no doubt. That is far from the end of it, however. Street names range far and wide, honoring Civil War battles, wildlife, the "Wild West," industrial production, Indian tribes, horse racing, European nobility (why, it would be difficult to say), theater terms, aviation parts, and many other categories in vast profusion.

Nostalgia for an old, non-Maryland home apparently moved some developers to hark back to names with little or no relationship to Maryland. Hence, a batch of South Carolina place names suddenly appears on the map in the middle of a secluded section, Glenside Park, between Harford and Belair Roads, just outside the Baltimore Beltway. Here are Santee, Pickens, Moultree, Pawley's and Saluda streets. Then, miles away to the northeast, just south of Bird River, are two memorials to important Dixie sea islands, Edisto (South Carolina) and Sapelo (Georgia) roads. For a sports-oriented community, Baltimore has surprisingly few

A typical ma and pa storefront of the nineteenth century, a hallmark of Baltimore streets.

sporty street names. There is an Oriole Avenue, an obscure way off the Windlass freeway at the head of Back River. There is also a Ruth, as in Babe, but alas, not named after the Sultan of Swat, for it is surrounded by streets that do honor to Veronica, Estelle, Carolyne and Marie. Gus Triandos, a famed Oriole squad member of the 1950s, gets a street. But there is no Baltimore Colt, no Memorial Stadium, and no Unitas Street, in or around town, though Pimlico (both a road and a street) is honored.

As a rule, exuberance marks suburban road naming, a sort of friendly and open-air Americanism, almost never nobby and unconscious of what might be laughable to the sophisticated. Most often, the name is only mildly jolting. Who would feel uncomfortable, for instance, dwelling in a small area just north of the beltway at Park Heights Avenue? Here the track reigns supreme, with Jumper's Lane and Pacer's Lane, where Tanner, Harness, Stirrup, and Fencepost courts house the faithful.

Wild West spirits took over when they laid out Oakdale, a neighborhood off Eastern Boulevard just east of the Martin airport. Here you will find Wagon Train, Covered Wagon, and Conestoga roads, with a Buckboard Lane and a Rodeo Circle thrown in for variation. As far as any local tie making names appropriate is concerned, it is usually nil. The names are strictly Duke Wayne in inspiration. It is a fact, though, that the

Conestogas visited western Maryland and old Baltimore in the grain market days 150 years ago.

The old Martin bomber plant once nearby seems to have started a trend toward informal street naming, very up-to-date for its day, on the eastern side of the metro area. "Aero Acres," a World War II-vintage housing development just west of Martin Plaza displays a wild profusion of aeronautical name-dropping. Fuselage Avenue, Propellor Drive, Cockpit Street, and Glider, Dihedral, and Hydroplane drives are among the entries.

Riding comfortably across Martin Boulevard to the northeast on (what else) Compass Road, the aeronautical riot continues at Victory Villa neighborhood. Here you will find a blinding assortment of airport and sky blue yonder street names . . . Slipstream, Taxi, Runway, Compression, Torque, Contact, Control, Supercharger, Altimeter, Strut, Airspeed, Manifold . . . almost all of them courts. Another section, Victory Villa Garden, continues the trend with such gems as the rather ominously named Tailspin Lane.

The great Indian tribes may be mostly a memory, but suburban streets remember quite a few. Blackfoot Court, Comanche Court, and Old Pawnee Road are included in the Village of Pawnee, another Martin area subdivision. The Valley Stream neighborhood, east and west of Greenspring Avenue near the city line, was even more generous with the fallen red man. Here you will find the Apache, Ozark, Blackhawk, Chippewa, Cherokee, and Navaho tribes remembered. Far out in the Deer Park area of the west side's Liberty Road, the tom-toms also sound for Shoshone, Pima, Ojibway, Yuma, Tuscarora, Hopi, and Chinook Indians. Somehow the tribes native to the Maryland region, the Piscataways and Susquehannocks, have been overlooked in this process. One wonders why. Perhaps the profuse naming of streets for Indians is more a tribute to the popularity of 1950s and 1960s TV westerns than to any geographical sense of U.S. history.

Many suburban county development people named streets to reflect a somewhat somnolent and peaceful air, "far from the madding crowd" as the poet once wrote. Hence the Pleasant Hill neighborhood above Owings Mills off Reisterstown Road features Gentlebrook Road, Softwoods Court, and Silent Glade

Road. Across the busy Reisterstown route, in honor of the once-popular straw hat theater nearby, the Morningside Heights community has named a Backstage Court, a Strawhat Drive, a Footlight Lane, and a Matinee Court.

At least two of the hundreds of newer communities in the area have striven for a touch of aristocratic class in street names. The residential area east of mainstream York Road near Padonia Road honors the Duke of Kent and the Duke of York with lanes. A Perry Hall area off Seven Courts Road pays tribute to your favorite friendly royal families—the Medicis, the Bernadottes, the Borgias and the Plantagenets. Just west of Woodlawn cemetery on the west side you will find a Duke of Windsor Court and a court honoring the Mountbatten family.

Another elaborate, upscale array of suburban street names appears in Queen Anne Village, a development in the Reisterstown Road corridor at Valley Road. Here we find that all the (English) stops have been pulled out. There's a Strand Court (as in London), a Wimbledon Lane (as in tennis), a Baroness Court, a Majestic Court, and a Royalty Circle. The two most famous English periodicals of the eighteenth century, the *Tatler* and the *Spectator*, are recalled in street names here.

Throughout the metro area, recently-dubbed regions are criss-crossed with arteries that have a more old-time, genuine ring, many of them colonial-era leftovers. Most all of them are roads, including Johnnycake, Whisky Bottom, Old Court, Spook Hill, Ward's Chapel, Lyon's Mill, Putty Hill, Pot Spring, Cromwell Bridge, and a hundred or so others. Here and there, almost poignantly, roads will reflect a lost era of industry, and even hard times. Such is the case with Cannery Avenue, Asphalt Avenue, and Wagon Street in Fairfield, a long-neglected industrial haven.

Sometimes street-naming will take a look back at an American event. In Middleborough off the Back River Neck Road, Antietam, the bloody, one-day western Maryland battle, is memorialized. The lesser known battle of the Monocacy river, in July of 1864, where General Lew "Ben Hur" Wallace held off the dastardly boys of Jubal Early's command long enough for Baltimore and Washington to wake up, is likewise remembered.

To be truthful, colorful names are greatly outnumbered by the thousands of streets that carry the names of girls and ladies, both young and old, or monikers suggesting suburban greenery, trees, and flowers, and, on occasion, wildlife. Carrollwood Manor, off Seneca Creek, is a riot of outdoors names. Routes honor the Blue Teal and Mallard ducks, along with Duck Blinds, and such amenities as Clear Water, Misty View, and Seawaves.

Streets in newer areas with bland names residents will vaguely associate with pleasant and outdoorsy habitats are endless. Oak, Pine, Willow, Beech . . . every conceivable tree, and most of the flowers as well, have been invoked to christen new residential routes. This made things nip and tuck at the zoning offices, which are unofficially charged with keeping out duplicates and spelling names correctly. Baltimore county appears to have been a bit sloppy in eliminating duplicates as the years of development and tract housing rolled past. Take the case of the trite name Edgewood. At least nine Edgewoods exist in the upper part of the metro area, two with street suffixes, five with road, and two with avenue after the name. Baltimore county officialdom actually passed three Edgewoods within walking distance of each other, and the county capital at Towson as well. The name Edgewater is similarly overused.

What every twentieth-century neighborhood street needs, and usually doesn't get, a Mr. Fixit shop. This storefront made the Historical American Building survey back in the 1930s.

When the vernal spirit takes over, however, it is not always hackneyed. The folks who built the southern end of Lansdowne on the southwest side of the metro area obviously lived the good, open, clean lifestyle. A bracket of happy names are found: birds, including humming, song and blue jay; plus lots of horticulture, with Winesap and Rambo apple streets. Nearby are streets dedicated to Gladys, Winifred, Hazel, Laverne and Marva.

What happy times, far from the heroics of earlier years, opening up such streets must have meant for 1950s and 1960s homeowners. They suddenly found the promise of the World War II song (a little plastic palace down in Dallas) coming true, as they had dreamed.

Each street was a record of affection. Roll back time to the tax-free 1890s, when men ran everything and watched their bank balances. Things were done in those days with great style by the wealthy.

Albert Blakeney had a bottle of champagne tucked away in his carriage and banker John S. Gittings, worth $2 million, stood beside him. Blakeney, chairman of the Baltimore county commissioners, and friends have gathered on upper York Road to christen a street. As yet, the route had not been named.

"Is there anyone here who wants to suggest a name for this new road?" asked Blakeney. "I think this road should be named Gittings Avenue," said the modest millionaire, adding that there was already a Gittings Avenue nearby that entered York Road. Why not continue it?

"Who donated the land and contributed the money to build this road?" demanded the county commissioner. "Why, Henry Walker, of course," Gittings answered. A nearby estate owner, Walker had underwritten the project to eliminate a detour from his property by connecting the new street directly with York Road.

"Well, that's the name of this road—Walker avenue!" declared Blakeney, as he shattered the champagne bottle on a culvert of the new intersection.

Despite the endless repetitions of trite name choices, something personal, political, or patriotic had gone into much of the city's street record since the earliest days. And sometimes the more personal christenings offer the most pungent illustration of the times.

In the 1950s, a surveying firm was laying out a new section in between a church cemetery and the east side of Fort Holabird, then a giant terminal for the U.S. Army quartermaster corps. They were right on deadline and were still stuck for one new street name. And you did not fool around and keep the U.S. Army waiting.

The day of the street name quandry also happened to be a Friday payday. The surveyor's go-fer and handyman, a fifty-three-year-old black war veteran from Virginia named William Hart, came into the office and sat down to wait patiently for his pay envelope. Like most engineers, these engineers had delayed the minor technicality of a street name until the last minute. All at once they noticed Hart waiting at the front of the office.

"Waiting for your envelope, William?" one of the bosses asked. Then, virtually in chorus, the men declared "It's Hartwait," and so it is to this day. The two-block street leads directly into Dundalk Avenue, Interstate 95, and the Francis Scott Key bridge, which takes travelers on south by the millions to Hart's native Virginia.

By the 1990s, the street-naming process had reached its 250th year. What had begun as a kowtowing to nobility and royalty was continuing in tributes to the common man and his necessities. So many times, the street story was one interlaced with honest efforts to survive. Many names reflected a touch of peace, along with endless tributes to Susan and Ellen and Debbie and Abby and Joan and all the rest. . . .

Names from La-La Land

The greatest single orgy of street naming in the metro area's history occurred from 1967 to 1980, when The Rouse Company was developing the planned city of Columbia in Howard County. While a few streets (Warfield Parkway, Harper's Farm Road, etc.) referred to local mores and names, dozens, perhaps hundreds, came out of the blue and inexhaustible air of la-la land. A few samples: Pushcart Way, Bullring Lane, Berrypick Way, Sleeping Dog Lane, Oven Bird Green, Timesweep Lane, Even Star Place, Fable Row, Ripplestir Place, and Drowsy Day.

The city's longest residential block, Wilkens Avenue. It stretches for more than 600 feet from end to end—more than 100 ''white steps'' on parade.

Streets

Of the approximately 15,000 or 16,000 streets in the greater Baltimore area today, only a tiny fraction were named before the American Revolution. But by the 1830s, virtually all the streets of the center city and the near east and west sides had been named. Some streets existed only on maps. The rapid spread of habitations and businesses was due to the financial shot in the arm the port got in the wars, both local and foreign, that left the city at times the only unexposed, functioning, large port of entry on the east coast of the U.S. Also important was the huge growth in the western Maryland grain economy and the building of economic links with western Pennsylvania.

From the 1840s through the turn of the century, streets and street names were most often created by wealthy entrepreneurs or venturesome builders. Beginning in about 1910, heavy industry and waterfront housing began to leap the city's borders and extend along hundreds of miles of Patapsco river frontage. Since the end of World War II, street growth has relied primarily on the more or less planned techniques of mixing suburban housing and shopping, as administered largely by county councils and planning agencies. Only rarely are imaginative design and strict conservation methods exhibited.

ABBOTSTON STREET
From the 2800 block of Kirk Avenue southeast

Lying just southeast of Memorial Stadium and a school with the same name, Abbottston's three blocks run from Harford Road to Kirk Avenue. The name remembers Horace Abbott, ironmaster and boss of the Canton iron works that rolled plates for Union ironclad boats during the Civil War, including, by legend, plates for the *Monitor*. "Abbotston," standing on the site of the present-day Baltimore City College building, was Abbott's home. It was one of the largest estate houses of its day, with mid-Victorian towers and a commanding situation.

ABELL AVENUE
From the 300 block of 30th Street north

Abell is a quiet setting of porched row houses that runs north and south through the Charles Village area east of Johns Hopkins University. In 1902 the city fathers named it after Arunah S. Abell, founder, in 1837, of the *Baltimore Sun*. The paper prospered on penny a copy sales, despite the competition of the far more powerful, and until later years dominant, *Baltimore American*. There's an Abell Lane, too, far up in Baltimore county near the village of Butler, and an Arunah Avenue, one block north of Edmondson Avenue near Gwynns Falls Park. Both may be dubbed in honor of the *Sun*'s founder.

AIGBURTH ROAD
From the 7900 block of York Road east

Baltimore streets named after nineteenth century estates come in bunches, and this is one of them. Called "Aigburth Vale," it was the home of the Bob Hope of his day, the vastly successful actor-comedian John E. Owens. The Aigburth mansion survives. The road runs from Stevenson Lane to York Road through a section called Donnybrook. Owens might have appreciated that.

AIKEN STREET
From the 1300 block of Lanvale Street east

Aiken runs through the light industry area of lower Harford Road below 25th Street. It probably is named after the Aikens (or Aitkens) of "Galen Hall," an estate founded by a Scotch doctor who fought on our side in the American Revolution.

AISQUITH STREET
From 1200 East Baltimore Street north

This very ancient route (it was named about 1804) used to be every taxi driver's secret way of getting downtown to the east side fast during rush hour. Alas, East Monument Street redevelopment has blocked its once unchecked and unknown path from 25th Street. It may be named for William Aisquith, merchant father of Capt. Ned Aisquith, whose gun squad killed General Robert Ross of the redcoats at the battle of North Point, Maryland, in 1814.

THE ALAMEDA
From the 2700 block of Harford Road northwest

The Alameda may sound like a shopping center that belongs in Kansas City, San Antonio or Pasadena. Actually, it's an attractive park-like roadway in the northeast city that begins at Clifton Park and links half a dozen quality residential districts, Ednor Gardens, Kenilworth Park, and Idlewilde among them, on its way to the city line and beyond. Originally it was part of a grandiose 1914 plan to link all the major city parks, including Patterson, Druid Hill, and Carroll, in a "grand boulevard" Paris-style. It was a plan that never came close to reality. Militant locals fought off an attempt to wreck The Alameda's magnificent forty-two-foot wide center strip, but had to sacrifice some width to traffic widening.

ALBEMARLE STREET
From the 800 block of East Baltimore Street southeast

Researchers believe this ancient little street (it parallels the Jones Falls in the eighteenth-century Jonestown district of downtown) may have been named for George Monck, Duke of Albemarle. He was the popular general who put Charles II back on the English throne in the seventeenth century at the end of the English Revolution. Albemarle exudes history—the Baltimore City Life Museums, a major tour stop, is nearby. It also bisects picturesque "Little Italy," with its parade of more than two dozen long-established Italian restaurants of village charm and heavy patronage.

ALICEANNA STREET
From 700 East Falls Avenue east

Hundreds of Baltimore streets are named for spouses and sweethearts. This hoary and historic route along the northwest harbor is one of the oldest of the breed. It's named for Aliceanna Webster Bond, a Quaker midwife who herself had ten children. Wife of John Bond, a Fells Point pioneer who with William Fell helped settle the district, she died in 1767.

ANELLEN ROAD
From the 3300 block of Dolfield Road northeast

The Ashburton area west of Druid Hill park includes this unusually named residential street. Anne and Ellen Placht had a big surprise coming back in 1941, when they were mere tots. Grandfather George W. Schoenhals announced he was naming a street in a new subdivision he was building after the two girls. Grandpa also named a road Bareva, after his two daughters, Barbara and Eva. "My daughters took the naming of their street in stride," Schoenhals told the press. "They smile when it is mentioned, that's all. But Anne and Ellen have been talking about theirs ever since I surprised them with it," the builder added.

ANNESLIE ROAD
From the 6600 block of York Road southeast

Both a pre-Civil War mansion, magnificently restored, and a neighborhood, Anneslie is named for the Harrison-Birckhead mansion that still stands. Frederick Harrison, a "gentleman farmer," named the original estate house after his daughter Anne. She married Lennox Birckhead, member of a wealthy landowning family of the Mt. Royal district. The mansion centers the small subdivision.

ARMISTEAD ROAD (AND WAY)
Southeast from Delmar Avenue

Armistead Gardens, the east Baltimore World War II housing project, with Armistead Way and Armistead Road, all note the services of Col. George Armistead. He was commander of Ft. McHenry during the British naval assault of 1814 that gave birth to the "Star Spangled Banner." Armistead Road is about seven miles southeast of Armistead Gardens in Edgemere, a water-bounded Baltimore county community.

ASHBURTON STREET
From 2700 Franklin Street north

Dan Webster, the Massachusetts senator, and Alexander Baring, Lord Ashburton, settled the interminable wrangling about the northern U.S. boundary between New England and Canada. This Walbrook area street is Baltimore's thanks.

ASHLAND AVENUE
From 900 Aisquith Street east

An upper east side street named for the Kentucky estate of Henry Clay, statesman and perennial presidential candidate (see introduction).

Rules of Thumb for Dating Homes

A streetwise fan in Baltimore who wonders how old the houses are can make rough guesses based on building types. Row houses with two and a half stories and dormers (or even one and a half floors) on old streets were built from about 1790 up to 1840 or a little later. Straight up three-story rows with decorative panels under the cornices were built from about 1830 until about 1910. If the windows are wide, the house is older; if they are long and narrow, they are probably mid- or late-Victorian; and if the windows and front doors are arched, they probably date from about 1880 to World War I. Single family rows, and row houses with porches facing the street, were built from 1850 through the 1920s. Stained glass windows and doors, and tiled roofs, were generally only used from about 1880 through the 1920s. The smallest row homes are only nine or ten feet wide, the largest rarely more than twenty-five feet.

AUCHENTOROLY TERRACE
From 2300 Fulton Avenue northwest

For some reason, west side place names have always had a somewhat peculiar ring (Alexandroffsky, Mondawmin, etc.). Probably none have been more tongue-boggling, to residents and visitors alike, than this one. The name's as Scotch as Haig & Haig pinch, though it sounds like some sort of battlefield in British India. A feature of the street, named after the estate of the Orem family, is a stately parade of very large, late victorian row homes with vast front porches. William Morris Orem named surrounding streets after poets (John Greenleaf) Whittier and (William Cullen) Bryant and an architectural critic, John Ruskin.

BAKER AVENUE
From the 5600 block of Johnnycake Road northeast

B

Baltimore county, with little regard for the headaches of the U.S. Postal Service, has opened no less than four Baker avenues. The one with the most visible history is in Westview near West Edmondale, named for Newton D. Baker, the harassed secretary of war in World War I. (Other officers of Woodrow Wilson's cabinet, and the president himself, also rate a street.) If your local postman is baffled, the other Bakers are in Parkville, east of Harford road, in Middle River in the shadow of the Eastern and Martin boulevard interchanges, and just off the headwaters of the Bird River. When they were building the Perry View section in Perry Hall, somebody slipped in a Baker Lane, also in the county.

BAKER STREET
From the 2200 block of Druid Hill Avenue southwest

It runs east and west through the heart of the city's west side, named for a wealthy family who owned a glass factory. Their home, "Friendsbury," near the eastern end of the street, was razed in 1905 when Monroe Street was cut through.

BALDERSTON STREET

Once a wide, truck-filled commercial alley that housed a wire works and other ventures, Balderston appears to have vanished under or near the forty-story tower of the United States Fidelity and Guaranty Company at Lombard and Light streets. The Balderstons were prominent nineteenth-century landowners. From 1793 until 1910 the family owned a variety of metal works marketing sieves, wire goods and hardware, plus fire screens and grillworks for cashiers' cages. Family property centered around the northern stem of Light Street.

BALTIMORE STREET
East and west from the unit block of Charles Street

This is the patriarch of all the streets in Baltimore; it apparently started life as Long Street, and then was called Market Street for years, though the present name dates as far back as 1745. In Baltimore parlance, a unit block is the first block of a given street up through ninety-nine if it goes that high. The hundreds are usually referred to as the first block.

Shiny-wet, but proud and happy, a band unit struts eastward down Baltimore Street (about 1930).

Baltimore Street is today, and was that long ago, the street that defines the city. It has never been out of style, and never anything but busy. Like many major streets in U.S. downtowns, it is forever re-inventing itself.

Hotels have hovered along this route almost since its beginning, for Baltimore Street is the natural human link between the harbor and the city. It races up and away over the hills of the west side, the slopes of Rolling Road, and Highlandtown.

One acknowledged architectural masterpiece survives along the way—the storied Art Deco masterpiece of the Maryland National Bank building. It was built in 1930 with twenty-eight working fireplaces for the offices of the city's business elite. The fire of 1904 wiped out the district but left the Alex Brown & Sons investment house, with its spalled stonework, safe from the great blaze. Re-use typifies Baltimore Street, east and west. On the oldest corner of the city, Baltimore and Calvert streets, have stood in succession, a theater-museum once operated by P. T. Barnum, the headquarters for a national railroad, a first class hotel, and today the highrise headquarters of a bank. For at least 150 years, parades have moved down the street east to wind up in front of City Hall and War Memorial Plaza. The street was named for Charles Calvert, Fifth Lord Baltimore, a typical self-indulgent Georgian aristocrat of the eighteenth century.

BANISTER AVENUE
From the 4800 block of Greenspring Avenue west

A tiny street that leads off Greenspring Avenue just west of Cold Spring, Newtown, it has a touching personal history. Charley Banister was "Mr. Foundation" of Baltimore building for twenty-five years, but was buried under a pit in a Raspeburg accident. He was crippled but recovered, and his builder, Elmer Ehrhardt, named the street after him.

BARNEY STREET
From 1800 South Charles Street east

One of a dozen streets that lead to Leone Riverside park in South Baltimore, it's named for Commodore Joshua Barney, who blew the English merchant fleet to smithereens in the 1812 war.

BARRE STREET
East from the 400 block of Sharp Street

There are two of them, one a vestigal affair opposite the new Federal Reserve center near the harbor, and the other a main stem of a renewal area. British Col. Isaac Barre was originally a French Huguenot refugee and one-time governor of Stirling Castle. He had been to North America and thought it was madness for Britain to attack a colony in 1776 that was twenty to thirty times the geographic size of the British Isles. Though he never visited the city, he was Baltimore's "kind of guy."

BAYARD STREET
From the 1300 block of Herkimer Street southeast

This street runs from the northeast border of Carroll Park virtually to the banks of the middle branch of the Patapsco River, a mile away. James A. Bayard helped negotiate the treaty of Ghent which ended the War of 1812.

BEAUMONT AVENUE
From the 5900 block of York Road east

One of the longer streets in Catonsville, the city's largest streetcar suburb, it bisects the northern section of the leafy suburb, running just south of Frederick Road (Route 144) north to old Frederick Road just south of U.S. 40 west. A second Beaumont in the city's Govans district is named for the estate of Ed Gans, a brilliant attorney, who turned down an appointment to the Supreme Court in President Taft's day.

BECK'S LANE
From Calverton Avenue west north of Hollins Street

This is a one-block street south of West Baltimore Street near the Gwynns Falls. Tom Beck was a small-time brewer and lived on nearby Calverton Road.

BEETHOVEN TERRACE
From the 100 block of Mosher Street to the
100 block of McMechen Street

An imaginative name given to the 1500 block of Park
Avenue in the Victorian Bolton Hill district, the
Beethoven is an urban set of townhouses largely converted into apartments. The great composer Ludwig
was the inspiration.

BELAIR ROAD
From the 2400 block of East North Avenue to
Bel Air, MD

Like parallel Harford Road, Belair is born at the old city
boundary, North Avenue, and takes off for the Gunpowder country and the Harford county seat at Bel Air.
Upper reaches of the route include some fine open
spaces, but the first fifteen of the twenty-two miles up to
Bel Air are often referred to as the "world's longest strip
shopping center," a bouncy, hilly affair with every suburban amenity. Belair can claim a "first" in street lore.
The first use of the innovative "Maryland shoulder," a
way of enlarging and paving arterial streets and highways, occurred here and on the Baltimore-Washington
Boulevard simultaneously in 1918.

An auto graveyard of the 1930s, probably off Belair Road.

BELLONA AVENUE
East and west from the 6300 block of North Charles Street

Wandering Bellona, which traverses some of the city's ritziest residential areas, is named for a powder mill that operated on the south bank of Lake Roland before the lake was filled. (The name refers to the Roman goddess of war, appropriate for a munitions operation.) Bellona is unique in the metro area for describing a horseshoe-shaped arc of easily fifteen or twenty miles. Returning to the same street, York Road, where it started, it has only one interruption, when crossing the Baltimore Beltway.

BENNETT ROAD
From the 1800 block of Eastern Boulevard northeast

Floyd Bennett, ace aviator, is remembered in this street that runs through an Edgewater neighborhood originally built to house aircraft plant workers.

BENSON AVENUE
From the 1000 block of Caton Avenue southwest

Benson is the main stem street that links Violetville with Arbutus and Halethorpe southwest of town. Oregon Benson, a powerful nineteenth-century politico and realty man, seems to have named the street for himself. He also added a street named for his son, Carville. There's an Oregon Avenue, also in Halethorpe, making the builder's presence a rare double-header in street naming.

BENTALOU STREET
From 2300 West Baltimore Street north, and
from Frederick Avenue south

Paul Bentalou came to America with Lafayette, fought
with Pulaski in Georgia, and became a successful merchant. With a few breaks, Bentalou runs from near
Druid Hill Park in the northwest city to Carroll Park on
the southwest side. It begins as a major node of black
education in the west North Avenue district, housing a
college, a major high school, a vo-tech center, and
primary schools.

BENTON HEIGHTS AVENUE
From the 4100 block of Moravia Road
northwest

The Gatches of Benton Heights were a land-grant family
with an estate that dated back to 1727. Thomas Benton
Gatch rode away to join Dixie in the 1860s and served as
a courier for Lee at Gettysburg. The family settled on
their Gardenville land in a big way; at one time there
were eight Gatch families living on Benton Heights land.

BENZINGER ROAD
One block south of the 3900 block of Wilkens
Avenue

The street runs one block south of Wilkens Avenue
(U.S. 1). The name is in memory of Harry M. Benzinger,
archdiocesan attorney for Maryland under Cardinal
Gibbons. Benzinger was a member of the board of a half
dozen major Maryland Catholic charities. Twice he was
received in private audience by Pope Pius XI. Cardinal
Gibbons performed the Benzinger's wedding ceremony
and the couple would often join his eminence in Gibbons' favorite indoor relaxation—the old-fashioned
game of euchre.

BESSEMER AVENUE
From 1400 Dundalk Avenue northeast

It honors Sir Henry Bessemer, the English metals inventor. It lies in two strips north of Fort Holabird Industrial Park. Bessemer's discovery of the converter process for manufacturing malleable iron and steel revolutionized English metals production by making processes less costly. In America, in partnership with William Kelly, Bessemer converters played a leading role in the manufacture of steel machinery, tools, wire, and structural members for the huge expansion of U.S. industrial capacity in the late nineteenth century.

BIDDISON LANE (AND AVENUE)
From the 3800 block of Echodale Avenue southeast

A 200-year-old political tradition lies behind the Biddison family. The lane honors the family's old neighborhood, as do extensions of Biddison as an avenue on both sides of Echodale Avenue in Gardenville. The Biddisons moved to Maryland from Virginia in about 1650. Abraham Biddison, a descendant of these settlers, fought the British in 1815. John S. Biddison, a Maryland assemblyman and a leader in the Southern Methodist church, was locked up for southern sympathies during the Civil War. His grandson, John, was a state senator; his great-grandson was a notable Baltimore city solicitor; and his son an assistant attorney general of Maryland.

BIDDLE STREET
East and west from the 1200 block of North Charles Street

The townhouse heaven of high society 100 years ago, Biddle nursed countless debutantes and aspiring mommas, including the mentors of a girl named Wallis, who was to meet an English king named Edward. Appropriately, the street was named for Catherine (Mrs. George) Lux, a Biddle of Philadelphia and wife of a Baltimore Croesus of the early nineteenth century who owned a 950-acre estate.

BLOEDE AVENUE
From 1400 South Cotton Avenue south

A short street near the city line in industrial Morrell Park, it is named for Victor Bloede, a German immigrant who cornered an obscure but lucrative market by making the world's best postage stamp gum.

BONAPARTE AVENUE
From 2400 Homewood Avenue southeast

The link between 25th Street industry and the Broadway corridor, Bonaparte is a reminder of the history of the Bonaparte's connection with Baltimore. The family heiress, Betsy Patterson, fascinated Napoleon I's brother and married him. Their children were not acknowledged by the great dictator (but were by Nappy's nephew, Napoleon III). The most useful American Bonaparte by far was Baltimore statesman Charles J. Bonaparte, a reform politician in Teddy Roosevelt's day.

BORN COURT
From the 200 block of Arch Street west

Herman Born was one of the countless German immigrants who enriched the city's intellectual life, industry, and crafts in the mid and late nineteenth century. He developed the biggest city wagon works in the post-Civil War period. Born Court is sited just behind the works that Born created. A Born Lane exists off Jones Road within Gunpowder Falls State Park.

BOSLEY AVENUE (AND OTHERS)
From the 400 block of West Joppa Road southeast

One can make the case that Bosley Avenue is Towson's most useful street, since it now routes traffic around suburban Baltimore's most congested area. On its way around, it passes the grounds of the county courthouse, whose land was donated in 1854 by Dr. Grafton Bosley. For some reason, county planners have sanctioned another Bosley Avenue, created far to the north off York Road in the Warren Road area. A Bosley Road is the main access road for some of the deluxe subdivisions fronting on Loch Raven Reservoir, and a Bosley Lane is a short street off Reisterstown Road.

BOULDIN STREET
From 3200 East Lombard Street south

A stop-start street, Bouldin begins to run almost due south off East Monument Street, jumps a few blocks to make room for Pulaski Highway, then continues to within a block or two of the Canton harbor. Jehu Bouldin was an early nineteenth-century surveyor (see introduction).

BOWLEY'S QUARTERS ROAD
From the 200 block of Carroll Island Road south

It's a central artery for access to hundreds of "shore" places washed by waters of the Seneca, Galloway, and Frog Mortar creeks, and for reaching Miami Beach Park. Dan Bowly (as he spelled it) was one of the harbor's first international shippers, active even before 1776. A Bowly's Lane borders Herring Run Park on the north, and moves north to cross the run into Mannasota Avenue.

BOYCE AVENUE
From the 6900 block of North Charles Street west

One of three streets that connect North Charles Street and Bellona Avenue through the secluded Ruxton area, Boyce takes its name from an Irish immigrant, James Boyce, who made a fortune in Cumberland coal as a result of the energy demands of plants and railroads in the Civil War.

BOYLE STREET
From the 700 block of Fort Avenue southwest

Off Fort Avenue in South Baltimore about halfway to Ft. McHenry, Boyle honors Thomas Boyle, who sank eighty enemy merchantmen (trade ships) and came home in 1815 with a million in loot.

Ten Street Corners Worth Remembering

West Baltimore and Sharp streets, where Congress Hall stood and where the Continental Congress gave George Washington almost dictatorial powers as commander in chief. . . . Fort Avenue and Wallace Street, entrance to Fort McHenry, whose star fort stood off the British fleet attack inspiring "The Star-Spangled Banner" . . . Pratt and President streets, where the Civil War opened in a vicious fire fight between militia and citizens, April 1861 . . . West Baltimore and Eutaw streets, where history's first inter-city telegraph message was received, in 1844, as Morse telegraphed from the Supreme Court, "What Hath God Wrought?" . . . Gay and Water streets, the Baltimore Exchange, where Abraham Lincoln lay in state . . . East Pratt and Albemarle streets, where Mary Pickersgill and other folk finished the original Star-Spangled Banner . . . Montgomery and Light streets where General Ben Butler and his small army arrived in May 1861, to secure Baltimore for the Union . . . Poppleton and West Pratt streets, site of the oldest railroad passenger station in the world . . . Preston and Howard streets, the 5th Regiment armory where Woodrow Wilson was nominated for president . . . Broadway and East Fayette streets, the Church Home and Hospital where Edgar Allan Poe died.

BROADWAY
From Thames Street on the harbor north

One of the city's widest streets, Broadway's upper stretches were once an elegant promenade. On its lower, harbor side, it gave birth to the town's east end retailing and wholesaling establishment. Now its lower stretches center on fashionable Fells Point, a sort of Georgetown with a Dublin accent. Broadway's most famous resident: The Johns Hopkins Hospital.

CALHOUN STREET
From the 2400 block of West Baltimore Street
north

Opened in 1836, Calhoun is a short, west side, north-south oriented street named for James Calhoun, the city's first mayor.

CALLAWAY AVENUE
From 3100 Garrison Boulevard northeast

Forest Park in the west end was founded in the 1890s by Frank Callaway, a realty investor. Handsome Callaway Avenue is one of its main arteries.

CALVERT STREET
From the 200 block of East Baltimore Street
north

Perhaps the most essential northbound street downtown, Calvert runs over the ancient Jones Falls marshes, long-ago filled in. Its Court Square and Battle Monument (to the 1814 heroes) are top historic spots. Up the street a ways is the home of the hoary *Baltimore Sun*. Luxury housing is returning to its mid-section. Calvert is unique in that it has a hospital at both its south starting point downtown and at its end off University Parkway. It also houses Center Stage, the city's nationally-known regional theater. The name honors the state's founding family.

CAREY STREET
From the 1200 block of West Pratt Street north
and south

James Carey was an early shipping and banking king of the city who favored popular elections and aid to black citizens. His memorial runs about thirty-five blocks, all the way from Carroll Park on the south to the old city border at North Avenue.

The old Calvert Street station where the Prince of Wales arrived for a tumultuous visit in 1860. It's flanked by the Grand Central Hotel, which catered to the Willie Lomans of the nineteenth century.

CARLTON STREET
From the 1100 block of Hollins Street north
and south

A jittery street that stops and starts, jumping near-west-side blocks near the Hollins Market, Carlton is named for Carlton House, the gaudy home of the Prince Regent of England (later George IV).

55

CAROLINE STREET
From the 1400 block of East North Avenue south

One of the east side's more endless rows, a north-south connector between North Avenue and Fells Point. Caroline was the sister of the last Lord Baltimore, Frederick Calvert.

CARROLL STREETS
From the 2000 block of Whistler Avenue northeast and southwest

The Carrolls were Maryland's richest family. One dozen streets begin with the name. The most historic is probably Carroll Street in Morrell Park, not far from the home of Charles Carroll the Barrister. His home, Mount Clare mansion, is the city's most elegant Colonial survival.

CARSWELL STREET
From the 2700 block of Kirk Avenue southeast

A four-blocker bordering Clifton park, the street is named for Robert Scott Carswell, one of the Canton district's early oil refiners.

CARTER AVENUE
From the 3500 block of Echodale Avenue northeast

A secondary street in Hamilton that runs northeast through what was once John T. Carter's strawberry farm.

CARVER ROADS
From the 700 block of Cherry Hill Road south

There are two. One is in the Cherry Hill neighborhood due south of center city, named in honor of George Washington Carver, the great black botanist and experimental scientist. The other is at Turner's Station south of Dundalk.

56

CATON AVENUE
From the 3200 block of Washington Boulevard
north

A major connector between U.S. 1 South and the
Irvington area to the north, and childhood home of
famed *New York Times* columnist Russell Baker, Caton is
named for Richard Caton, the inept son-in-law of
wealthy Charles Carroll the Signer. Caton failed miser-
ably in several major ventures and went into bank-
ruptcy, not something easy to do when your father-
in-law is one of the richest of Americans.

CATOR AVENUE
From the 4000 block of Old York Road east

This short street in northern Waverly is named for the
nineteenth-century *modiste*, hat stylist, and major milli-
nery store owner, Robinson Wesley Cator.

CAVENDISH WAY
From the 6300 block of Boston Street north
and south

Pioneer chemist Henry Cavendish, who discovered the
components of water, is remembered, along with other
famed scientists, in streets within the World War II
vintage housing development of O'Donnell Heights.

CHARLES STREET
From Winder Street, South Baltimore, to Lincoln
Avenue, Lutherville

If there is a *grande dame* in Baltimore's street world, the
title goes without contest to Charles Street. But once you
admit this, you have to add that the old girl has "really
lived." Charles bisects the Baltimore world as Broadway
does New York City, as the Seine River does Paris; and
it has been doing this for two and a half centuries. Its
downtown stretches date from the days of King George
I. Its southern tip dips its toes into the salty water of the
Patapsco, and its northern terminus, ten and a half miles

The city's oldest street spectacle, the annual spring flower mart sponsored by the Women's Civic League in historic Mount Vernon Square.

from the harbor, runs through country that still has a few building lots for sale.

Classy retailing, world science, uppity club life, big money, college education, and urban planning have all found Charles a hospitable environment, but so have senior citizen homes and modest blue-collar housing. It bisects the skyscraper district downtown, but is also an encyclopedia of historic U. S. building styles. The most photographed item in the metro area, next to the ancient U.S.S. *Constellation* afloat in the harbor, is Mount Vernon Place, gifted with a column in memory of Washington. The lavish town houses of the Mrs. Astorbilt period and two of Maryland's greatest treasures, the Peabody Conservatory and the Walters Art Gallery, are also prime tourist attractions. Charles Street offers another "must" tour stop as it passes Homewood Mansion, home of Charles Carroll, Jr., dating from 1803. It's part of the campus of Johns Hopkins University, which is, from the standpoint of projects funded, the U.S. government's number one private scientific research resource.

CHASE STREET
From the 1000 block of North Charles Street east and west

Chase features the Belvedere Hotel, a major ornament of the Mount Vernon area. Considered the "Plaza" (as in New York City) of Baltimore, it is a millionaire-built fantasy of French Renaissance extravagance, constructed in 1901.

CHATHAM STREET
From the 2000 block of East Preston Street south

A short block just south of East Preston Street that recalls William Pitt, Earl of Chatham, who cheered Americans on in their quarrel with England.

Samuel Chase, a Maryland founding father, was a legal storm center. The street with his name is a midtown institution.

CHEAPSIDE STREET
One block east of South Calvert Street near Water

A tiny way in the north harbor whose name may have been inspired by a London (England) duplicate.

CHESTON AVENUE
From the 3500 block of Walbrook Avenue north

A short block bordering public schools in Walbrook, Cheston was named for a wealthy shipping family and an early ornament of that family, Galloway Cheston, a pal of Johns Hopkins and George Peabody.

CLAGETT STREET
Originally near Fremont Avenue and West
Franklin Street

Heroes of the seige of the city in 1814 are remembered in
a cluster of Locust Point streets near Ft. McHenry. Lieut.
Levi Clagett was killed in the "rocket's red glare" attack
on the fort. His memorial street was far to the northwest, destroyed in the drastic clearance of the Franklin-
Mulberry corridor.

CLAY STREET
From the 200 block of Liberty Street west

It's a hilly, one-block affair leading up to Preston Gardens, just north of center city, that continues for a few
more blocks on the other side of Charles Center. Though
they never much liked Henry Clay (they preferred
fire-eating Democrats), Baltimoreans named this street
for him sometime before 1842.

CLEVELAND AVENUE (AND
STREET)
From the 1100 block of West Cross Street
southwest

Not every U.S. president rates a street, but Baltimore
loved Grover. His street is in the near southwest city,
near Carroll Park. The avenue is in Brooklyn near
Chesapeake Avenue.

CLINTON STREET
From the 3300 block of East Monument Street
south

It runs for miles due south through East Baltimore and
into the reviving, once-industrially-mighty Canton area
out to Lazaretto Point, a one-time quarantine house on
the harbor where interstate traffic tunnels north and
south, twenty-four hours a day.

COKESBURY AVENUE
From the 2200 block of Homewood Avenue east

A short street just east of Greenmount Avenue near North Avenue, it was named in 1910 for the Methodist divines Coke and Asbury, at the behest of a local church.

COLGATE AVENUE
From Dundalk Avenue east to the city-county line

Dick Colegate came to America from Britain in 1697, already over fifty years old and rated as an old man. The Baltimore county climate and land dealings agreed with him. He wheeled, dealed, and got rich. A Dundalk Avenue connector is named for him, though spelled more simply than the seventeenth-century original.

COLLINGTON AVENUE
From the 2200 block of East Baltimore Street north and south

It runs through the center of the massive grid that is east Baltimore, from Collington Square off East Preston Street south to the harbor area. There's another loop of the street that ends a few blocks north of the square after crossing Gay Street. The origin of the name is obscure, but Collington was the name of an important tract in the organization of Prince Georges County in the 1690s.

COOK'S LANE
From Exit 91 of Interstate 70 to Edmondson Avenue

It sounds tiny and unimportant, but it isn't. It connects the Social Security district with U.S. 40 west. John Cook (born Koch) emigrated from Baden, Germany, in 1853. A nurseryman and rosarian of monumental note, he was the first American to produce a hybrid tea rose.

COOLIDGE AVENUE
From the 1000 block of Haverhill Road south

For some reason Democratic Baltimore snuggled up to silent Cal Coolidge, our most reticent chief executive. In 1927, while he was running the Oval Office, the city named his street. It's in Violetville near U.S. 1 south.

COPPIN COURT
One block northeast of the Bethune and Bunche road intersection

Fanny Jackson Coppin was the first black woman to graduate from an American college. Her name was given to Coppin State College, a unit of the University of Maryland. Her street is in Cherry Hill, the 1940s planned community south of the Hanover Street bridge.

CRADDOCKS LANE
From the 100 block of Greenspring Valley Road south

An important suburban residential street, Craddock links Valley Road with upper Reisterstown Road. The name honors a family that spelled it Cradock, who came to the country about 250 years ago and lived at an estate house, called "Trentham."

CRAIG AVENUE
From the 700 block of Beaumont Avenue south

Slave owner Dr. John Craig, born at the end of the eighteenth century, was one of the original Baltimore-Florida commuters. He maintained a home facing York Road at Woodbourne Avenue, in Govans. His porticoed home has vanished, but Craig Avenue remains near the old homestead north of Tunbridge Road.

CRITTENTON PLACE
From the 800 block of West 32nd Street south

An inconspicuous street overlooking the Jones Falls in Hampden, Crittenton remembers New York-born Charles N. Crittenton, who founded a Baltimore home for unwed mothers.

CULVER STREET
From the 3700 block of Old Frederick Road north

The wealthy Culvers of Chicago bankrolled many famous social service institutions, including Hull House. They also were among the nation's earliest sponsors of home ownership for the poor. Helen Culver, of that family, is remembered in this street that runs northeast from Old Frederick Road to link up with Hilton Street.

CURIE WAY
From the 6300 block of Boston Street south

Madame Curie, the co-discoverer of radium and its properties, is recalled in this O'Donnell Heights residential street.

CUSTER ROAD
From the 3700 block of Wilkens Avenue southeast

George Armstrong Custer, the Civil War hero and Indian campaign flunkout, is remembered in this tiny, one-block street between Wilkens Avenue and Southwestern Boulevard.

CYLBURN AVENUE
From the 5000 block of Pimlico Road east

The wealthy Tysons, philanthropists of black causes, owned "Cylburn," a castellated Victorian estate, now center of a large nature study haven. The street runs from the park westward to Pimlico Road.

63

DANIELS AVENUE
From the 3200 block of Taylor Avenue, northeast and southwest

President Wilson and his cabinet have memorial streets in the metro area. One of them, off Johnnycake Road east of Catonsville, is in a section where the president and other cabinet members, including Josephus Daniels, Navy secretary, are honored. Another Daniels Avenue crosses Taylor Avenue from near the city line into the county in northeast Baltimore. A Daniels Road in eastern Howard county leads to a Patapsco mill site of that name.

DECATUR STREET
From the 1300 block of Fort Avenue northeast and southwest

Locust Point's riot of patriotic and military names from the early nineteenth century (Towson, Beason, etc.) includes a tribute to Stephen Decatur, who went to the shores of Tripoli and declared "Our country, right or wrong!" There's also a Decatur Road in the Victory Villa section of Middle River east of the city.

DEWEY AVENUE
One block west of the 4200 block of Evans Chapel Road

An almost invisible one-block street in northern Hampden off Roland Heights Avenue, Dewey is named for the wildly popular admiral, George, of the Spanish American War. Like Cal Coolidge, Dewey "did not choose to run" for president.

DOBLER AVENUE
From the 3300 block of Harford Road northwest

With a son in real estate, it was no trick of fate for popular, modest Judge John J. Dobler to rate a street. It would never have occurred to the judge to want one, however. The city thought he did, and Dobler was duly named just before World War I. It's a short street overlooking Lake Montebello on the northwest side.

DOLFIELD AVENUE
From the 4700 block of Garrison Boulevard southeast

This is an important northwestern area route in town that links the attractive Arlington and Ashburton residential areas. Alex Dolfield, a banking exec turned realty investor, is honored in the name.

DOOLITTLE ROAD
From the 100 block of Back River Neck Road northeast

Bouncy, smiling World War II ace Jimmy Doolittle, the scourge of Tokyo, is remembered in this small street that bisects Back River Neck Road near Josenhans Corner.

DORIS (AND AUDREY) AVENUES
From the 4000 and 4100 blocks of 6th Street, Brooklyn

The Mewshaws of Baltimore have done well being remembered in city streets. When dad, Clinton, subdivided the family farm in the 1920s, he named daughters Doris and Audrey on the street plan. He also named nearby streets Franklin Avenue, after his father, Franklin Mewshaw, and Townsend Avenue, after his secretary, a Miss Townsend, the latter act possibly a Baltimore first. There is another Doris Avenue off Philadelphia Road in Rosedale, and an Audrey avenue off Joppa Road in Carney.

DOUGLASS COURT
One block west of the 300 block of North Caroline Street

This is a small street near the intersection of Broadway and Orleans Street, an honoring gesture to Frederick Douglass, the great black orator and nineteenth-century abolitionist who learned to read in Baltimore as a youth.

DREW STREET
One block north of the 6100 block of Eastern Avenue

Dan Drew was one of the slipperiest Wall Street customers who ever graced New York, but he also invested in Baltimore's Canton Company. In a 1918 annexation the firm, large east side landowners, christened the street in Drew's name. It is just west of Key Medical Center and leads into and across Eastern Avenue.

DRUID HILL AVENUE
From the 600 block of North Howard Street northwest

This street, along with parallel McCulloh Street and Madison Avenue, is one of the legal, cultural, and social capitals of black history. More than 150 years of Baltimore efforts in black education and civil rights, and the efforts of resident families, the Mitchells and Jacksons among them, found a home in the Druid Hill region. The avenue, when first opened, was scorned as a mere carriage way for rich whites of the 1860s.

DUCATEL STREET
From the 2300 block of Eutaw Place northeast

A two-block affair in northwest Baltimore's Reservoir Hill district, Ducatel links elaborate Eutaw Place with more modest Brookfield Avenue. Jules Ducatel was a chemistry professor who headed the University of Maryland's chemistry department in its earliest years.

DUKE ALLEY AND DUKER COURT
West of the 100 block of North Central Avenue (alley)
The 400 block of President Street east (court)

Duke Alley is a short street just north of Pratt Street on the east side. The court is a series of six blocks that weave in and out of the east side on the margins of Little Italy and Fells Point. The court recalls Otto Duker, a German immigrant lumberman whose "Christmas garden" promotion at his plant included ice ponds and waterfalls.

Curious Lore

By 1909, street cars were carrying 530,000 people every day over 400 miles of track.

DULANEY VALLEY ROAD
From the 100 block of East Joppa Road north

This major suburban artery escapes, almost as if relieved, from Towson into the open country of north Baltimore county, passing Goucher College and running a winding route through some of the state's most desirable residential homesites. It expires near Manor Road more than eight miles north of the city. It's the namesake of Dan Dulany, the state's best-known pre-revolutionary attorney.

DUMBARTON AVENUE
From the 200 block of Rodgers Forge Road northeast and east

This street runs from York Road west to Stevenson Lane north of Rodgers Forge. It takes its name from the Greek revival Taylor-Rieman mansion built in 1853. Since the mid-1950s it has been the property of the Baltimore county board of education. A Dumbarton Road also exists in Waverly east of York Road.

EARHART ROAD
One block northwest of the 1700 block of Eastern Boulevard

Amelia Earhart vanished into the Pacific Ocean in 1937, after many widely publicized airplane flights. Her memorial is in the once-major aircraft manufacturing center of Middle River.

EDEN STREET
From the 1300 block of Federal Street south

It starts at the north harbor in the old City Dock area and runs due north almost to North Avenue. The route is cut short by a few interruptions, including the Dunbar High School complex and redevelopment housing off Central Avenue. Sir Robert Eden, the last (and most popular) royal governor of Maryland, is honored.

EDGAR TERRACE
One block southeast of the 4800 block of Walther Avenue

A business associate dubbed this street in honor of C. Edgar Wood, builder of thousands of home units, and a kingpin of the Hamilton area. There's also an Edgar Road far distant on waterbound Turkey Point in Baltimore county.

EDISON HIGHWAY
From the 3300 block of Erdman Avenue south

Famed inventor Thomas A. Edison is namesake for this road, a largely industrial route that links the Belair Road district with Highlandtown and the harbor through the Highland Avenue extension.

EDMONDSON AVENUE
East from Chalfonte Drive, 3 blocks west of the 2200 block of Old Frederick Road

This anchor of west side city traffic is actually a remnant of historic Route 40 west to Frederick, Maryland, the Baltimore National Pike—one of the nation's earliest attempts at a national highway. It misses becoming the pike at the city line, moving on to hook up with Interstate 70 in Howard county. Dr. Thomas Edmondson, who inherited wads of money his pa had made in the 1790s Baltimore merchant boom, was the city's first major art collector. In 1876, the city fathers honored him by changing the name of long-established Thompson Road to Edmundson. Edmundson peels off east of Catonsville to proceed through a dense residential district before dead ending at Chalfonte Drive at the Catonsville Middle School.

EIERMAN AVENUE
From the 4400 block of Belair Road northwest

J. George "Doc" Eierman was a home contractor who learned the wagon wheel trade as a young man. They called him Doc because he always carried a little black bag. Inside the bag was no stethoscope, but a bathing suit and towel for swimming sorties. His street is a short one, moving northwest from Belair Road to just beyond the Herring Run.

ELLIOTT STREET
From the 1100 block of South Conkling Street west

Elliott Street real estate has blossomed in recent years because of the rapid "gentrification" of stable Canton, the north harbor home community. In the area, formstone fronts now blend with elegant "mews" put up to take advantage of the boom. Jesse Duncan Elliott was an early-nineteenth-century figure continually involved in duels. He died peacefully in 1845 as the super of the Philadelphia Navy Yard.

ELLWOOD AVENUE

From the 3000 block of East Baltimore Street north and south

This street has a good residential run through the east side's Canton and Highlandtown neighborhoods, then is chopped up into pieces just east of Baltimore cemetery. Harry Storck, builder, named the street for a friend, businessman L. Ellwood O'Connor about 1905, a decision made while chatting on a porch in Govans.

EMORY STREET

From the 600 block of Washington Boulevard north

This picturesque nineteenth-century street might go unnoticed were it not for the fact that it was the home stamping grounds of America's all time No. 1 baseball great, Babe Ruth. The Babe was born in what is now his museum in the 1890s (though his parents lived on nearby Camden Street), and it has been meticulously restored. Local and national fans have expanded the baseball memorial to cover the history and legends of the Baltimore Orioles. Ruth's parents ran a saloon on nearby Camden Street, and, by an accident of history, the site of the saloon will become short centerfield of the new Oriole stadium, underway at this writing.

Babe Ruth's memory and the history of the Baltimore Orioles are part of the show at Emory Street's Babe Ruth Museum. The Babe was born in the building when it was the home of his grandparents.

ERDMAN AVENUE

From the 3200 block of Harford Road southeast

The Erdmans were early German immigrants who became pillars of east side farming when there was still open country on the east side. Erdman Avenue is now a major artery leading from the far south Clifton Park area to link up with Interstate 95 and North Point Road.

ESSEX STREET
From the 2100 block of Fleet Street east

The oldest street in town by this name is a short three-blocker that carries traffic to and from Canton's waterfront. But there's an Essex street, road, and lane, too, respectively, in the northern Essex area of the far east side, in Woodmoor on western Baltimore county turf, and in the Carriage Hill development off Liberty Road.

ETHELBERT AVENUE
Two blocks northeast of the 5300 block of Park Heights Avenue

This Pimlico area street, just southwest of the famed race track, was christened in 1903 by an early settler. Charles H. Green took the unusual route of simply picking a name, painting a sign, and putting it up. The name he picked, Ethelbert, was a contraction of the names of two of the family's daughters, Sarah Ethel and Alberta May. City officials recognized the street name as official in 1918.

ETTING STREET
From the 500 block of Dolphin Street north

It parallels Pennsylvania Avenue from the North Avenue area to the margins of downtown. This street honors Solomon Etting, Baltimore grandee and early sponsor of the Baltimore & Ohio railroad. He was the first Jew elected to public office in Maryland after a long-standing Jewish disabilities law was repealed in 1825.

EUTAW STREET
From the 300 block of West Baltimore Street north and south

Long a major element in west side business, Eutaw for years was second only to Howard Street as a nineteenth-

and early-twentieth-century shopping area. Jewelry, photography, and dry goods and chinawares were some of the offerings. Eutaw House, a Union headquarters during the Civil War, was already famous when the boys in blue moved in, for from one of its rooms history's first telegraphic message was sent by S.F.B. Morse. To the north it becomes elegant Eutaw Place, a grand Victorian promenade. The street is named for a Revolutionary War battle that starred John Eager Howard, local hero.

Collapse of the Wanderlust Department

You can't really blame people for settling down and taking it easy after fighting traffic, ferrying school kids, and listening to 80 or 90,000 TV commercials. Folks have put it in writing by naming streets. There's a Dunroming Road in the Cedarcroft-Idlewood area just north and south of Northern Parkway. Dunrovin Lane is a short street at Philadelphia Road near White Marsh. Dunloggin, a major subdivision built by a former lumberman, is in northern Howard County. And there's a Dunrobbin Court in Anne Arundel County, doubtless an encouragement to the local residents.

EVESHAM AVENUE
From the 5700 block of Northwood Drive west

Evesham links the Chinquapin parkway area on the east with Govans on the west. It is named for the Johnson-Clemens mansion, a distinguished house of the Gothic revival style that was hauled away in dump trucks in the 1960s. Some pieces of the notable interior survive in other residences.

FAIRMOUNT AVENUE
From one block south of 1100–1300 East
Fayette Street east

The best known Fairmount in the metro area is an old east-west artery on the east side. It mounts one of the tallest city hills and produces one of the best views. Heavy renewal activity has brought this street back near the Johns Hopkins Hospital. At mid-century it was a sort of Baltimore Hell's Kitchen.

FAIT AVENUE
From the 800 block of South Montford Avenue
east

It's an unchanging slice of row house living for the first mile or so of its route, from the edge of Fells Point to Highlandtown. It leapfrogs through industrial sections and a defunct cemetery, disappearing and then reappearing for two more miles before terminating in Baltimore county, about five blocks from the city line. The name honors William Fait, a giant in the seafood canning business. He would employ 600 workers at his Canton plant, then be forced to shut down when Eastern Shore plants, using cheaper labor, cut prices.

FALLS ROAD
From the Jones Falls bridge exit and Lafayette
Avenue entrance north

The historic and winding Jones Falls border road is lined with nineteenth-century mill relics, picturesque stone architecture and expensive real estate. Along with Fells Point and the Patapsco River mill country, it helped to found Baltimore.

FAYETTE STREET
From the unit block of North Charles Street
east and west

Washington's aide, Lafayette, inspired two streets and a square in Baltimore. The most visible is Fayette Street, a compendium of eastern urban lifestyles; it has highrise swank, urban renewal inner city, blue collar suburb, and townhouse grandeur in a four-mile run directly through downtown east to west. Parallelling it about half a mile north is the less urban Lafayette Avenue, largely residential in character. With a bit of leapfrogging, Lafayette makes it all the way to the east side's Baltimore Cemetery. Fayette Street gives access to Franklin Square, and Lafayette Avenue to Lafayette Square, among the noblest nineteenth-century survivals on the west side of town.

The 1828 shot tower on East Fayette Street, said to have been the tallest structure (234 feet) in the U.S. when built. Note cobblestones.

FILLMORE STREET
From the 1100 block of East 30th Street north

The obscure president Millard Fillmore, who moved into the White House when Zach Taylor died, is the inspiration for the three short blocks of Fillmore that border an elementary school in the old Homestead district. It was laid out in the nineteenth century west of Harford Road.

FLEET STREET
One block south of the 700 block of Eastern Avenue east

Fleet Street is one of the longest and busiest of all routes on the lower east side, and one of the oldest. Its picturesque earliest section, which reaches the inner harbor, predates the American Revolution; the far eastern sections are a main stem of neat, durable Highlandtown. Nobody knows absolutely where the name came from, but the shipping industry and its link with London are good guesses.

FOERSTER AVENUE
From the 2600 block of Hollins Ferry Road southeast

It's spelled Forester Avenue on some maps, but the name goes back to a painter-saloonkeeper who emigrated to the U.S. in 1864. William and wife Augusta prospered, and Foerster's son John named the new street for dad.

FORT AVENUE
From the 1400 block of Race Street east

Fort Avenue is the ceremonious approach to the Ft. McHenry national monument. It runs from the village and residential style of South Baltimore, making an abrupt change past the heavy industry and separate community of Locust Point. Both areas are generally breezier and cooler than anything else so close to center city and the avenue rides high and straight on its peninsula, as if somehow proud of its triple role as defender of the city (in 1814), rebel lockup (in the 1860s), and giant hospital nurturing tens of thousands of sick and injured back to health during and after World War I.

A Sunday outing at Fort McHenry about 1880.

FRANKFURST AVENUE
From South Hanover Street east and southeast

An important access road to the outer harbor waterfront community of Fairfield, Frankfurst is a contraction of the name Frank A. Furst, a German immigrant who rose from the role of tobacco stripper to politico of state-wide prominence. In private life he was an equally potent executive of Baltimore's huge grain shipping operations.

FRANKLIN STREET
From the 400 block of North Charles Street
east and west

Westbound Franklin Street, and its eastbound twin a block south, Mulberry Street, are the traditional and only partially adequate east-west routes through midtown. Both funnel heavy traffic on both sides of what many regard as the city's top architectural achievement, Benjamin Latrobe's Basilica of the Assumption, begun in 1806. Also cradled in the gap between the two routes is the central Pratt Library, created over a hundred years ago by Enoch Pratt, a hardware king of the era, as the city's first public library system. Surprise: Franklin Street is not named for the great Ben of Boston and Philadelphia, but for one Thomas Franklin, who was a presiding justice of the city in later life. He also helped out in a 1747 resurvey of the city.

FRANKLINTOWN ROAD
From the 2600 and 2700 block of West
Baltimore Street south and north

It loops picturesquely off of Edmondson Avenue (U. S. 40 west) through interesting nineteenth-century remnants, then dives into the glades of Leakin Park to the far-off Woodlawn area beyond the city line. Franklintown, possibly named for Ben, was a far west side hamlet that was headquarters of the western Maryland butchering trade.

The cast of one of the Keystone Cop shows rests by a Maryland roadside while on location for the National Film Corporation early in the twentieth century.

FREDERICK ROAD (AND STREET AND AVENUE)
From the 1600 block of West Baltimore and Gilmore streets south and west

It's fairly simple. The avenue becomes the road fairly near the city line, and the road continues on toward its namesake destination, Frederick City, as Route 99 in Howard County. The street is a dinky, ancient block on the east side of the central business district.

FREMONT AVENUE
From the 800 block of West Baltimore Street north and south

Modern construction of Martin Luther King Jr. Boulevard, and the Franklin-Mulberry Street rebuilding of U. S. 40 have interrupted Fremont's once lance-like path from the old south side to the northwest side's Upton district, where it ends near a new subway station. The route is widely accented with nineteenth-century architecture. As a west side feature, it honors John Charles Fremont, the pre-Civil War western explorer, California explorer, and military man.

G

GARRETT AVENUE (AND OTHERS)
From the 900 block of East 25th Street north and south

Whatever else you may say about them, the Garretts of Baltimore, onetime owners of the now extinct, once great Baltimore & Ohio railroad, have plenty of name memorials around town. The main one and probably the oldest, Garrett Avenue, is close to John Work Garrett's nineteenth-century estate of Montebello on the northeast side. But there's a Garrett Road near the Maryland line, a street in northwest Brooklyn, and another Garrett Avenue bordering Arbutus Memorial Park.

GAY STREET
From the 2300 block of East North Avenue south

The great Italian Gothic tower of the old No. 6 Engine house, built in 1853, is the most famous symbol of this well-known, now cut-up industrial street slicing diagonally across the oldest part of the northeast side. A major renewal effort in the 1970s turned Gay's midsection into a restyled pedestrian mall, anchored by a residential highrise. Another spellbinding street scene created in the 1700 block is the Victorian fantasy (some might say nightmare) of the old American Brewery building. It's been vacant since 1973, but it's still a fun aggregation of scary, hooded architecture of the Alfred Hitchcock school of design. The street name honors Nicholas Ruxton Gay, who helped lay out the town in 1747.

GERNAND ROAD
From the 1900 block of Kenway Road, Mount Washington, west

Ed Gernand was a prosperous citizen who enjoyed being generous to others. About 100 years ago he settled in the Dixon Hill section of Mt. Washington near the city line, drilled for water, and came a gusher. He shared the water with neighbors and organized the local water company. He also lent his pond to churches for local baptisms and published a community bulletin. The road was christened in 1911, the year Ed Gernand died.

GIBBONS AVENUE
From the 5400 block of Harford Road northwest

This street helps define the southern margins of the Hamilton district of northeast Baltimore. It honors James Cardinal Gibbons, the legendary Catholic prelate who marched behind the casket of Abraham Lincoln as a young priest. He went on to six decades as a beloved figure of the Baltimore scene. There's also a Gibbons Road leading east from York Road to the Dulaney Valley Memorial Gardens.

GILMAN TERRACE
From the 500 blocks of West 33rd and West 32nd streets east

One of the city's streets that fronts on a park, Gilman Terrace dates from 1920. It looks east from the slopes of Wyman Park west of the Johns Hopkins campus. It recalls the university's first president, Daniel Coit Gilman.

GILMORE STREET
From the 1600 block of West Baltimore Street north and south

A long, straight, north-south street that helped shape the giant grid that is west Baltimore, Gilmore is probably named for the wealthy Gilmor family—Robert, the original merchant prince, or his son, the art collector. Probably not honored in the name is Harry Gilmor, the rebel captain who swept through northern Maryland in mid-1864 on an extensive raid. Historians think that someone, perhaps the city records office, garbled the Gilmor family name when the street was laid out. There's also a Gilmore Avenue in Woodlawn near Gwynn Oak Park.

GIST AVENUE
From the 3800 block of Strathmore Avenue
south

This street runs about a mile northwest from Hayward Avenue in Pimlico to Strathmore Avenue south of Pikesville. General Mordecai Gist, who fought the battle of Camden (South Carolina) in the Revolution, was the namee. A native Baltimorean, he spent the last years of his life in sunny Charleston.

GITTINGS AVENUE
From the 5900 block of North Charles Street
east

Gittings begins opposite the grounds of the ultra-select Elkridge Hunt Club, rolls along nicely through the Pinehurst residential area, and ends at York Road. Richard Gittings, the family's prominent criminal lawyer, was honored in the naming. A short street in the middle of the South Baltimore peninsula also bears the Gittings name.

Can You Spell That, Please?

Street namers have enriched the "how's-that-again" tradition in greater Baltimore with some real show-stopping names. How about Wind Song Way, Sister Pierre Drive, Sling-Ora Drive, old Nike Missile Site Road, Niner's Private Road, Obsidian Drive, Sue-Dan Road, and Dark Head Road.

GLADSTONE AVENUE
From the 5100 block of Roland Avenue east

A slice of horse and buggy America in Roland Park that honors the glowering, practically immortal old snoop and British prime minister, William Ewart Gladstone. Most famous local resident: James Bready, Oriole historian and baseball sage.

GLEN CURTIS ROAD
Two blocks northwest of the 1700 block of
Eastern Boulevard

It's a couple of blocks north of Eastern Boulevard between Middlesex and Edgewater. Some there remember the days during the 1910s when Baltimore air shows pioneered the art of flying. The street misspells the name of mega-pioneer Glenn H. Curtiss, the "first man to fly a mile," and the designer of the Curtiss Jenny used in World War I. Neighboring streets are dubbed in honor of other air heroes.

GORMAN AVENUE
From the 2300 block of West Baltimore Street
north

This tiny street intersects arterial Fayette Street far out on the west side of town. It was named for Senator Arthur Pue Gorman, longtime Democratic state boss of Maryland politics late in the nineteenth century. Regarded as a political wizard in the league of James A. Farley of the Roosevelt years, Gorman served twenty-four years as a heavyweight in the U. S. Senate.

GORSUCH AVENUE
From the 2600 block of Harford Road west

This street links busy Harford Road with equally busy Greenmount Avenue, running south of Memorial Stadium. Old timers call the district Homestead, after the name of the original Gorsuch estate, dating from 1736. At one time, family holdings totalled 7,500 acres.

GOUGH STREET
From the 200 block of Central Avenue
southeast

This street name is pronounced "Goff" by many locals, not "gow." Harry Gough of "Pery Hall" plantation donated the name. He was one of the wealthiest Marylanders of the 1780s. Methodist Bishop Francis Asbury converted him from Episcopalianism and he figured in the founding of Methodism's constitution at Baltimore's Lovely Lane meeting house. Gough begins at Central Avenue on the edge of the downtown and leapfrogs several miles in five stop-and-starts that end at Canton Industrial Park.

GOVANE AVENUE
Just east of the 5000 and 5600 blocks of York Road

Govans is one of the most recognizable in-city neighborhoods of Baltimore, a country town with a long history, now surrounded by city. Few locals, however, know that the name Govans comes from a forgotten Scotch landowner of the Colonial era. He became the heir of a wealthy father in 1763, but James Govane would not survive long enough to produce an heir. He died in 1783 with no male descendants. "Govane's town," as the village crossroads was first known, became the nineteenth century's "Govanstown," a community of 500 lining both sides of York Road. Govane is a short street east of York Road and south of Benninghaus Road.

GREENE STREET
From the 500 block of West Franklin Street south

One of the quickest ways of getting out of town southbound, busy Greene Street's claim to fame is that it is the spine of the huge University of Maryland professional school and hospital. The medical faculties' shock trauma unit used in accident rescues is world famous. Greene is believed to honor General Nathaniel Greene, Revolutionary commander in the bitterly fought southern campaign.

HAMILTON STREET
East and west of the 500 block of North
Charles Street

It's a picturesque, alley-sized assembly of old coach
houses and other remodeled dependencies that runs
east and west from St. Paul Place to Park Avenue.
Informal mens and womens clubs are set up in two of
the older buildings. There were plenty of local Hamil-
tons to inspire this street name, but holdouts still vote
for founding father Alexander.

HANLON AVENUE
From the 2500 block of Ellamont Street east

Ned Hanlon, legendary manager of the 1890s' Baltimore
Orioles, sometimes called "the father of modern baseball," hits a double-header out on the northwest side
with both a park and street carrying his name. Hanlon
Park wraps around Lake Ashburton south of Liberty
Road. Hanlon Avenue reaches the lakefront at Longwood Street.

HANOVER STREET
From the unit block of Lombard Street and the
100 block of Barre Street

Though Baltimore patriots killed the name German
Street during World War I, they left South Baltimore's
Hanover Street intact, though it represents the German
province that gave birth to four rather dumb King
Georges of England. Hanover for years has been one of
the least charming and most obviously fallen of major
local routes into town. Now, with a possible boom in
shore property around its long bridge, and the revival
underway in South Baltimore, better days may be
ahead.

Hanson Avenue recalls the country's first president, from Frederick county, John Hanson.

HANSON AVENUE
From the 6200 block of Greenspring Avenue west

It's named for Revolutionary notable John Hanson, first president of the United States in Congress assembled under the Articles of Confederation of 1783. It runs two blocks in northwest Baltimore off Greenspring Avenue. Marylander Hanson presided over the national assembly as it was before the revision of the government under the Constitution in 1787. In the mid-1780s the U.S. was a confederation of states.

HARDING PLACE
From the 700 block of 34th Street south

Though a flunkout as Republican president, for some reason Harding was highly popular in died-in-the-wool-Democratic Baltimore. He came to town in 1922 to dedicate the Key Memorial at Fort McHenry. In his honor, two blocks being developed in the southern Hampden area were named for him. There's also a Harding Street among a group of presidentially-named streets in Timonium Hills, and a Harding Avenue in Carney.

HARFORD ROAD
From the 1400 block of East North Avenue north

Named long ago for the county to which it leads, Harford Road is the umbilical cord that ties the Hamilton district, with its family-oriented homestyles, to the rest of Baltimore. Taverns and gas stations are scattered here and there, but the minute you step off the main drag, it's all tomato plants in summer and Christmas gardens and lights in winter. There are also two Harford avenues in town, one in Catonsville Manor on the west side, and one in the Oldtown section of the east side near the Maryland State Penitentiary.

HARRISON STREET

Downtown's Harrison Street used to go under water regularly during freshets of the Jones Falls. It was virtually swept away in an 1868 deluge. That problem was solved when the lower falls were routed through a giant culvert. Originally, the humble little street was named for wealthy Thomas Harrison, who brought his money with him when he came to town in 1742. Now Harrison seems to have disappeared in the elaborate redevelopment of Market Place, and the extension of Interstate 83 exits. There's an avenue in Middle River and a road, named for William Henry, among other presidential streets in Fairway Park west of Ft. Holabird. These insure that the Harrison name, from Baltimore's social register, will not pass away overnight.

HAYWARD AVENUE
From Winner Avenue at Pimlico Racetrack southwest

With his partner, David Bartlett, Jonas Hayward built an international metal fabricating business. The avenue, a considerable affair that goes southwest from Pimlico race track to the Wabash Avenue district, bisects Hayward's country property.

HEATH STREET
From Leone Riverside Park west

Heath leads to Leone Riverside Park in South Baltimore. It was named in 1820 in honor of Maj. Richard Key Heath for his battlefield bravery at North Point, September, 1814.

85

HECKEL AVENUE
From the 3700 block of Parkside Drive
northeast

In 1895, Charley Heckel, son of a masonry contractor, started a home section which was at the time far remote, north of Herring Run Park. In 1902, he named a street there for himself, a one block affair adjoining Holy Redeemer Cemetery.

HERBERT STREET
From the 1900 block of Poplar Grove Street
east and west

Approximately one Marylander in three donned the Confederate grey in the Civil War. One of these was Confederate commander James R. Herbert of Ewell's command. He was wounded at Culp's Hill, Gettysburg, captured and exchanged for, and fought again at Petersburg. His street runs four blocks north of west North Avenue in Walbrook.

HERKIMER STREET
From the 1700 block of De Soto Avenue
southeast

Herkimer Street runs through the southern and central part of Morrell Park in southwest Baltimore. The name was drawn from the battle career of New York's General Nicholas Herkimer, Revolutionary commander. In an odd sequence, the street appeared on maps in a Carroll Park location from 1822 until 1859, then it disappeared for a while, only to reappear about a half mile to the south in 1880 at its present location.

HILLEN STREET AND ROAD
From Ensor Street south of Monument Street
to Holliday Street

Hillen Street is a major in-bound traffic artery that takes westbound traffic into Calvert and St. Paul streets downtown. Hillen Road in the north end begins at Harford Road just south of Lake Montebello, and ends at Loch Raven Boulevard more than a mile away, just north of the city line. The terminus is near the country seat of the politically active early-nineteenth-century pair, Solomon and Thomas Hillen. At thirty-two, Solomon was the youngest mayor ever elected in the city.

HILTON ROAD AND STREET
From the 3300 block of Liberty Heights Avenue north and south

Often confused with Hillen (to the anguish of visitors and cab drivers), Hilton is a main north-south lateral on the city's outer west side. It links Ashburton with Frederick Avenue and the southwest city. It continues north of Liberty Heights as Hilton Road to connect with busy Wabash Avenue and the city subway route. The name almost certainly derives from the 1,000 acre estate, "Hilton," summer home of slippery, snobbish William Wilkins Glenn. The wealthy Glenn was a Confederate subversive who ran a sort of underground railroad in reverse, smuggling rebel sympathizers and British officers and nobles south into Dixie. One of his customers was the future Duke of Devonshire.

HOLABIRD AVENUE
From the 2000 block of South Newkirk Street east

Holabird Avenue is one of the few city streets named for a professional army man. Honoring Sam Holabird, a West Pointer and Civil War brigadier, the name also graced a fort, the huge Fort Holabird army quartermaster's depot. Today the land is being recycled as an industrial park. With Soller's Point Road and Merritt Boulevard, Holabird forms a triangle inside of which is Dundalk Community College.

HOLLIDAY STREET
From City Hall Plaza north

It's always had a somewhat theatrical air, and still does, since War Memorial Plaza has been fitted out with a stage for informal concerts. It defines the grandiose stairway entrance of the Baltimore city hall, built in 1876. John Robert Holliday was "high sheriff" of Baltimore County in the early days. The street opened in 1783.

Curious Lore

By 1942, only eight lived-in private houses survived below North Avenue in the Mount Vernon district.

HOLLINS STREET
From the 800 block of Parkin Street east and west

A showcase of Victorian renewals, Hollins is most famous as the lifelong home of H. L. Mencken, 1920s critic and professional curmudgeon. Hollins Market is the oldest community market in the city, and one of the oldest in the U.S. Union Square is a beautiful nineteenth-century remnant. The 800 block, headquarters for the city's Lithuanian culture, is an outdoor museum of architectural styles.

HOMELAND AVENUE
From the 4700 block of North Charles Street east

David M. Perine built the lavish "Homeland" estate in the Greek Revival style in pre-Civil War years. Today's street borders the campus of the College of Notre Dame of Maryland, with its noble stands of nineteenth-century oak and poplar trees. The single-family home section, also called Homeland, that has developed to the north of the avenue is one of the most select in the city, with distinguished 1920s and 1930s buildings.

HOOPER AVENUE
From the 200 block of Druid Park Drive north

William E. Hooper was the city's cotton mill king. He also created the Hampden-Woodberry communities of the nineteenth century, placed in the virtual center of town. His namesake street runs around a hill that houses the studios of two of the town's three television stations. Additional Hoopers exist downtown near the Baltimore Customs House, and in southwestern Baltimore county off Wilkens Avenue.

HOPKINS PLACE
From the unit block of West Lafayette Street south

The very name had a ring of horror about it in this century. Hopkins Place was where the terror started in February of 1904, when the downtown burned. Before that, Hopkins meant gold, for Johns Hopkins was by far the town's richest man. There are four other Hopkins; a plaza that is part of Charles Center downtown, a lane serving as a route in a ritzy subdivision near Garrison in north Baltimore County, an avenue in Lansdowne, and a street in Rodgers Forge.

HOWARD STREET
From the 200 block of Camden Street north

Once the heart of city retailing with four department stores, Howard has become a minor office center with a major subway stop. Unchanging amenities include the town's biggest antique row and the enormous Lexington market. The market is one of the nation's major fresh food centers in a day when such things have disappeared from Paris and New York. Howard is named for John Eager Howard, Revolutionary soldier, also memorialized in John and Eager streets.

With three streets in his memory, (John, Eager, and Howard), the general, hero of the Revolutionary brawl at Cowpens, South Carolina, is the all-time triple-header in city street naming.

An enormous warehouse flame believed to be near the start of the fire.

Fighting the fire in the central business district.

The type of fire wagon that answered the call to the fire of February 1904.

Where the fire stopped, near Lexington and St. Paul streets. The massive courthouse on the left saved mountains of city records.

The south side of stately Court Square (with 1814 monument at left) still smoking after the 2,000 degree roasting.

A hose company dampening burned-out shells in the blaze.

Only trolley tracks and a few poles are left on street site.

The first restored service in the fire aftermath, trolleys on blackened street corners.

New dock houses went up, but the bulkhead (at left) remains desolate.

Unique before and after photos, probably never before published. West Baltimore Street looking east from Liberty before rebuilding began, and three years later in 1907, after clearance and revival of trade.

HUBNER STREET (AND AVENUE)
South of 36th Street between Beech Avenue and Keswick Road

A short block in east central Hampden, the street is named after German immigrant John Hubner, who landed at the harbor at age fifteen and built up a home construction business. Many of his houses still stand. Hubner moved to Catonsville, where his home was a few blocks from present-day Hubner Avenue.

HUGHES STREET (AND AVENUE)
From the 700 block of South Charles Street west

This may be the only Baltimore street dedicated to a man whose works are museum pieces. Christopher Hughes was an artist, crafting silver pieces in the 1770s and 1780s. His street near the west harbor feeds busy Hanover Street traffic. The avenue is off Jones Creek south of Edgemere.

HULL STREET
From the 1400 block of East Fort Avenue north and south

Captain Isaac Hull, captain of the U.S.S. *Constellation* in 1812, inspired the naming of this one, part of a cluster of heroes so honored around Fort Avenue, Locust Point.

HUNTINGTON AVENUE
From the 300 block of West 29th Street north and south

A main artery of the blue collar area north of 25th Street near the falls. The name dates from a tract originally surveyed in 1688.

94

HUTSCHENREUTER LANE (AND ROAD)
From the 12200 block of Harford Road south and east

Baltimore, while it has always had classy retailing of porcelains and art china, is not known for fine china manufacturing. So what is this famous name from Selb, Germany, doing out in the middle of nowhere near the wildlife in and around Cone Scout Reservation and the Gunpowder Falls? Who knows? All that seems certain is that the great Hutschenreuter kilns (founded 1814) are still churning out superb stuff, and that a plate with the Duchess of Devonshire's picture on it is $325, according to recent antique books.

HUTTON AVENUE
From the 4900 block of Windsor Mill Road south

The Gaun Huttons of Baltimore and Newport, R.I., were disgustingly rich from money she inherited from the Winans family (railroad kings for the czar of Russia), and old Hutton money. They lived in a giant "Alexandroffsky," a towering west-Baltimore mansion that closed in the 1920s with a marathon auction of contents. The Huttons also owned "Crimea," a summer palace in Leakin Park. Hutton Avenue leads into the park today. There is also a Hutton Place, and another stretch of Hutton Avenue just to the west of the park in Windsor Terrace off Windsor Mill Road.

IBSEN AVENUE
South of Holabird Avenue and east of Newkirk Street

The stark, lonely Norwegian author and great playwright, Henrik Ibsen, is remembered in this short, stark and lonely little avenue off Newkirk Street in the Canton railhead district.

ILCHESTER AVENUE
From the 2800 block of Greenmount Avenue west

Ilchester is an ancient town in southwest Britain and a Maryland country village, but this Ilchester is a small, two-block way in the Homewood section, east of Johns Hopkins University. It's also a road south of town off Montgomery Road in Howard County, and a street way down south in Anne Arundel County near Deale Beach.

Curious Lore

Canary Court, just east of Patterson Park, is only one-fourth of a block long—but nine houses, dating from the 1890s, were built there, each ten to eleven and a half feet wide.

INCINERATOR ROAD
Four blocks east of Ordnance Road east of the Arundel Expressway

Good old Anglo-Saxon describes this street off Solomon Road. It dead-ends at the Baltimore & Ohio railroad tracks near Curtis Creek in Anne Arundel County.

INVERNESS AVENUE
From the 1500 block of Forest Hill Avenue northeast and southwest

This very Scotch name pops up in Morrell Park off Washington Boulevard near the city line. (In Scotland, it's the place where Macbeth is supposed to have done in Duncan.) English names abound in the district, including Sexton, Whistler, James, Gloster, and Whittington, indicating a literary-minded surveyor (even if he misspelled Gloucester.) Anne Arundel County has an Inverness in the Riverdale-Sunset Knoll section on the Magothy's west bank.

IRVING PLACE
One block southeast of the 4800 block of
Manor Road, Dulaney Valley

A cul-de-sac in the swank and well-named Long Green Valley subdivision called Dulaney Valley estates—also a road linking the old and new Frederick roads opposite Loudon Park Cemetery and Mount St. Joseph College.

J

JACKSON STREET (AND ROAD)
From the 600 block of East Fort Avenue north and south

Old Andy rates two streets in the city, one in the county: a street on the east side of the oldest part of historic south Baltimore, a road deep in the Beaverdam country north of the city, and another, Jackson Road, included in a wild series of tributes to early U. S. presidents, that parallels Sollers Point Road near Dundalk Community College. Not certainly inspired by the president, but perhaps, is a Jackson Avenue off the Governor's Highway (Route 3) and a Jackson Lane off Solley Road in the Stonehaven section of upper Arundel County.

JEFFERSON STREET AND COURT
From the 400 block of North Highland Avenue east

It runs east and west from Johns Hopkins Hospital to Highland Avenue and also serves as a remnant block west of the hospital in a renewal area. The counties have remembered the founding father, too. Baltimore County named an avenue in Timonium and a road in the Academy Lane subdivision between Owings Mills and Reisterstown; Anne Arundel County named a place; and Howard County named a street.

JOH AVENUE
From the 3900 block of Wilkens Avenue southeast

This important local street links Benson Avenue and Violetville with Morrell Park. Louis Joh was a local magistrate who went into building and land development with family land bought when the Duchess of Leeds auctioned tracts she had inherited from the Carrolls of Carrollton long ago.

Solid rubber tires and a solid rubber look from the city engineer, posing with new equipment at the foot of the Washington Monument. The paving blocks are Belgian imports, legend says.

JOHANNSEN STREET
From the 1200 block of Pennsylvania Avenue
east

A short, one-block street near the old Northwestern police station where Paul Johannsen (1870–1931), an 1888 Baltimore arrival from Germany, was a notable magistrate. He learned English by working on a German-language newspaper and studying law.

JOHNSON STREET
From the 200 block of East Heath Street north
and south

It's the west border of Leone Riverside Park in south Baltimore. Edward Johnson was an early mayor, the first political "boss" of the city. The street was his first and apparently only memorial, for the elementary school facing the park is named for a different man, a Thomas Johnson.

KAVON AVENUE
One block southeast of the 3500 block of Belair Road

Frank Novak was the Henry Ford of the early-twentieth-century Baltimore building industry, managing crews that built about 10,000 city homes. He was a nattily dressed man who became well known around town, since he bore a distinct resemblance to President Woodrow Wilson. He forbade any surveyor or company employee to name a street after him. But Glenn Smithson, a colleague, dared—or almost dared. Kavon (Novak backwards) went into the record books, and Frank said, "Well . . . you finally put one over on me!"

KELLY AVENUE
From the 5900 block of Greenspring Avenue east

Back in the years when people commuted north to heavily treed, diverse Mt. Washington, Simon Kelly was working his way up from a railroad section gang to a crossing watchman at the suburban station. Everyone knew him for his lavish use of Anglo-Irish from the "oulde coontree." Everyone called the street that ran from the Jones Falls Hollows up the hill Kelly Avenue. When Mt. Washington was annexed to the city, the informal name became official.

KELLY PLACE
North of 38th Street near the Falls Road intersection

A tiny street off Falls Road in Hampden is thought to be named for Martin Kelly. One hundred and fifty years ago, he was the Irish-born magnate of the area when it was called Slabtown, for the shape of rocks used in building its homes. Martin and son John were the builders, and the Hampden community might well have ended up as Kellyville or Kellytown. The Kellys were strong supporters of the Catholic church and helped build the local sanctuary. When it came time to give a permanent name to what is now Hampden, an ironic choice was made. City fathers chose "Hampden," the name of an estate nearby. The estate was named for John Hampden, English revolutionary, who opposed the English Catholic church and who, with Oliver Cromwell's followers, took over the English government and axed King Charles I.

KENNEDY AVENUE
From the 1100 block of East North Avenue north

Not JFK, but one Capt. William Kennedy, whose "Oak Hill" estate was a pre-Civil War showplace in the neighborhood, inspired this street. It has two dog-legged sections, one a dead end at The Alameda, another on the northeastern corner of Greenmount Cemetery. Kennedy was rescued from a Gulf of Mexico storm, and in thanks built St. Ann's Church at Greenmount Avenue and 22nd Street. He founded the Mount Vernon Cotton Mills, a firm that a century after his death was still recognized as one of the most profitable and best-managed companies in the United States.

KENSETT STREET
From the 2500 block of Francis Street southwest

Tom Kensett is to the canning industry what the Wright brothers were to aviation. A New Englander of inventive mind, he created the modern canning industry on Baltimore turf, got rich, and built a mansion on nearby Pennsylvania Avenue. Kensett Street bisects the southern part of his nineteenth-century estate.

KEY HIGHWAY
From the 600 block of Light Street east and south

This very visible inner city route leads directly to the inner harbor and center city off Interstate 95. It passes the south shore of the inner harbor, destined to become a glittering array of residential highrises. The road's honoree is Francis Scott Key, the Washington attorney who wrote the national anthem after watching the rockets' red glare and seeing that the flag was still there.

KIERLE COURT
Just east of Amity Street two blocks north of Fayette Street

When Washington crossed the Delaware river and sent the hated Hessian mercenaries flying, one of the captured was a Dr. Heinrich Keerl, an educated German. Keerl decided America was a better deal than back home and founded one of the city's earliest drugstores. Over the years the family name was subject to various spellings; surveyors of the nineteenth-century settled for Kierle, a short street on the old near-west side.

KIPLING COURT
From the 800 block of East Belvedere Avenue southwest

It all depended on Mrs. Pistorio. Her husband, Sam, was putting up single-family houses in a new section just off Belvedere Avenue in the Govans section. The little cul-de-sac was as yet nameless, but the Pistorios were fans of the rugged English storyteller, Rudyard Kipling. "Why not Kipling Court?" asked Mrs. Pistorio, and so it was.

KOLB AVENUE
From the 6400 block of Belair Road east

It straddles the city-county line just west of Belair Road, a memorial to one Henry Kolb, homebuilder. He put up hundreds of houses in the Belmar-Overlea district early in the twentieth century. Nearby Madeline Avenue is named for Kolb's daughter. In his way, Hank Kolb was a philanthropist for his own and future generations. He would sell a house for $35 down, with payments of $2.50 to $3 a month, until the mortgage was paid off.

KOSSUTH STREET
From the 3700 block of Old Frederick Road northeast

While not particularly left-wing itself, Baltimore has always loved a real revolutionary hero, from Washington on down. This short, dog-legged street (it links Old Frederick Road with Hilton Street) is a memorial to Louis Kossuth, the Hungarian patriot who came to town in 1851. Admirers came from miles around, and his visit gave birth to a special Baltimore dessert, made in his honor and pushed by an enterprising local baker. The "Kossuth cake," a layered ice cream cake with chocolate frosting, is still served occasionally around town.

KRESSON STREET
From the 4100 block of East Monument Street south

An east-side industrial artery, Kresson begins on East Chase Street, and below Monument Street works in tandem with southbound Haven Street to funnel traffic on both sides of railroad trackage. Relatively short, it complements access roads including three of the major east-west routes, Monument Street, Pulaski Highway (U. S. 40 east), and Eastern Avenue.

L

LANDWEHR LANE
From the 2300 block of Frederick Avenue north and south

Just west of the west end of Pratt Street, and north of Frederick is Landwehr Lane, yet another monument to a hard-working German. John H. arrived in 1832, a mere child. His dad disappeared, and he went to work in a hog bristle factory when he was six or seven. Profits from a grain mill set him up in the business of home development. When his neighborhood was annexed in 1888, the city named a street for him.

LANGLEY ROAD AND STREET
Three blocks northwest of the 1700 block of Eastern Boulevard

Samuel P. Langley, an aeronautical great, has a major memorial in the famed Virginia airfield, but his pioneering is also noted in Middle River's Langley Road. A Langley Street is near Mount Winans in the Hollins Ferry Road area.

LANIER AVENUE
From the 2500 block of Oakley Avenue north, Pimlico

This street is the southwest border of Sinai Hospital in Pimlico. It honors Sidney Lanier, the Georgia poet, who spent eight years in Baltimore before his death from tuberculosis at age thirty-nine.

LANVALE STREET
From the 1700 block of North Charles Street east and west

One of the more select addresses in heavily restored Bolton Hill. Lanvale continues westward through the Fremont Avenue corridor, into the hillside of Harlem Park, Baltimore's oldest "urban renewal" area and eastward to the Patterson Park district. The name is probably of Welsh origin.

LATROBE STREET
From the 300 block of East Lafayette Avenue
south

The Latrobes, beginning with the great Anglo-American architect, Benjamin, made major contributions to the nation. Ben's grandson, Ferdinand C. Latrobe, was seven times mayor of Baltimore between 1875 and 1893. The family street is west of Greenmount Avenue in a heavily deteriorated district.

LAURENS STREET
From the 1200 block of North Monroe Street
east

Laurens begins at Park Avenue in the upper Bolton Hill district, then heads due west for about a dozen blocks west of Fremont Avenue to Monroe Street. John Laurens, of Charleston, South Carolina, one of Washington's most aggressive field officers, is honored in the name.

LAWRENCE STREET
From the 800 block of East Fort Avenue
northeast

Locust Point boasts this memorial to John "Don't Give up the Ship" Lawrence of the U. S. Navy. There's also a Lawrence Road in Dundalk and two avenues, one south of Roland Park and another off Pulaski Highway in Rosedale.

LAZEAR ROAD
South from Franklintown Road west of
Weatheredsville Road, Gwynns Falls

This is a quiet by-way in leafy Gwynns Falls Park. It is named for a great medical hero, Dr. Jesse W. Lazear. He offered his life in the experiments in Cuba, at the turn of the century, as doctors worked toward conquering yellow fever.

LEADENHALL STREET
From the 1200 block of Ostend Street north
and south

A street in one of the city's oldest industrial districts,
Leadenhall may be named after a famous London business street. The Baltimore version dates from 1811.

LEAKIN STREET
From the 2200 block of Boston Street
northeast

The all-powerful Canton Company, harbor developers,
named this street off Boston Street for Sheppard C.
Leakin, a hero of the 1814 fight and former city mayor.

LEE STREET
From the 500 block of South Hanover Street
east and west

One of the oldest lanes in the west harbor area, Lee runs
west from Light to Sharp streets. Richard Henry Lee,
Virginia statesman, inspired the name.

LEMMEL AVENUE
From Kennison Avenue south to Groveland
Avenue

This short street borders an elementary school property
in the Arlington district. It's named for William H.
Lemmel, who presided over one of the brightest eras of
city public education from 1946 until his sudden death
in 1953.

LEXINGTON STREET
From the 200 block of North Charles Street
east and west

Lexington's most interesting blocks were partially destroyed in clearance work for the Charles Center project

in the 1960s, including two theaters and a magnificent Belle Epoque bank. It survives as a pedestrian mall; it is also a valid example of a nineteenth-century west side rowhouse street, and serves as the south side of quaint Franklin Square.

LIBERTY HEIGHTS AVENUE
From the 2600 block of Reisterstown Road northwest

A main northwestern artery, born at Mondawmin Mall and moving through the upper west side to become Liberty Road at the city line. Quality subdivisions of the early twentieth century and the suburban campus of the Community College of Baltimore line the route.

Liberty Street in the mid-nineteenth century, with firehouse and cathedral spires.

LIBERTY ROAD
From the city line at Flannery Lane Road northwest

It follows an ancient Conestoga wagon path to Frederick county via Libertytown, a storybook hilltop village, but for young Baltimore it is the yellow brick road to better housing. Generations have leapfrogged to home ownership along it. Its home styles run from highrise cliff to garden balcony and flattop ranch, with a sprinkling of the newly fashionable Victorian manse with porch.

Curious Lore

In October of 1872, disaster struck—an epidemic hit the equine population and all horses died. People either walked or stayed home.

LOMBARD STREET
From the 100 block of North Charles Street east and west

Lombard Street rushes through downtown Baltimore westbound as if someone or something was in hot pursuit. It is today, and always has been, a hot commercial artery through the center of town. The namesake is lost to history, but may have been a counterpart street in London.

Though in some stretches it is a forty-mile-an-hour truck and car parade, it has housed all sorts of life in two centuries; cigar plants, factory lofts, courts, government offices, and religious centers. To Baltimoreans it means "corned beef row," a handful of delis that purvey what many think are the best pastrami creations of the middle Atlantic. Two superbly restored synagogues that were the focus of Jewish life in the pre-Civil War period and a new Jewish historical museum form a unique testament to immigrant life in nineteenth-century America. Another attraction on Lombard's western reaches is the "Bromo Seltzer Tower," a replica of a Tuscan city hall, once topped by a bottle of the antacid as big as the tower and nightlighted for extra impact.

LUERSSEN AVENUE
From the 3900 block of Southern Avenue
southwest

It's a five-block street just east of Most Holy Redeemer
Cemetary in Gardenville. War veteran Charles H. Luerssen was murdered in 1921 in his dad's grocery store.
Seven years later, his father, while building some houses
on the family homestead off Moravia Avenue, unexpect-
edly named one street Luerssen Avenue, either after his
son or himself or the family. He never told anyone who
he was honoring.

MADISON AVENUE (AND STREET)
From the 800 block of North Charles Street east and west

One of the main stems of the old northwest side near Druid Hill Park, Madison marks the western boundary of the Reservoir Hill renewal district, an architecturally varied section that has resisted both renaissance and total decay. Below North Avenue, Madison is a thoroughfare for Maryland state employees and the city's state government center.

As it nears downtown, Madison becomes a street and heads due east through Mount Vernon, passing Johns Hopkins hospital on the near east side. Robert E. Lee made his home on the western reaches of the street about 1848.

MALSTER AVENUE
Just east of the 1500 block of Mount Royal Avenue at McMechen Street

A tiny street behind the promenade of Mount Royal Avenue named for the city's thirty-first mayor, William T. Malster, marine engineer and shipbuilder.

MATTFELDT AVENUE
From the 4600 block of Falls Road south

If there's a slice of Archie Bunker America in the city limits, it's this porch-front, how-dee-doo sort of place, all but buried in a midsection of the Jones Falls. Stable and unassuming Mattfeldt breathes a 1940s and 1950s ambience, a place of wading pools, kayaks and canoes, boat tows, and jungle gyms. Carl L. Mattfeldt, a West Baltimore Street jeweler, founded the neighborhood in 1865. Son Otto went into building homes on both Mattfeldt Avenue and Sabina Avenue, the latter street was named for Mrs. Otto Mattfeldt. Otto's son, Col. C. L. Mattfeldt, won the Distinguished Service Cross in World War I. His son, John P. Mattfeldt, won the D.S.C. in World War II, and gave his life in the European war theater.

A $1 million gift to the city from Enoch Pratt, hardware millionaire, launched the city's public library system in the 1880s. Until the 1930s, this was the Pratt Library's central branch building, a pile of granite on Mulberry Street, razed when the new building was opened.

MAYNADIER ROAD
From the 400 block of Oakdale Road south

A leafy residential street from the *Meet Me in St. Louis* period of domestic living, it recalls a fruit farm by that name that stood on the site (and shipped pears to Philadelphia) long ago.

McCABE AVENUE
From the 5200 block of York Road east

Larry McCabe was a Lehigh University man who made it big in railroad engineering by designing much of the New York subway system. He lived year round in north Baltimore, however, and when they opened up a street leading to his rural home, he named it for his family. Larry Jr. was a jockey and won the 1921 Kentucky Derby on Old Rosebud. The street runs east from the endless Greenmount Avenue-York Road stem in Govans.

McCULLOH STREET
From the 2500 block of Cloverdale Road, Druid Hill, south

McCulloh fuses with Druid Hill Avenue just southwest of Druid Hill Park. Its solid, mansion-sized rows have long been home to black gentry. Nobody is sure of the name's origin. It's named after either James McCullough, famed nineteenth-century actor, or James McCulloh, a bank officer who figured in the famous *McCulloh v. Maryland* case, which asserted the federal government's immunity from state tax.

McDONOGH STREET AND ROAD
From the 1700 block of East Chase Street south

The street is an east side affair running a few blocks south from Biddle to the Kennedy Children's Center of

112

Johns Hopkins. The road is a substantial suburban route linking Reisterstown and Liberty roads. John Mc-Donogh, a New Orleans banker and abolitionist, said to be the largest landowner in the U. S., is honored in the name. McDonogh founded a school in his name in Baltimore County.

McELDERRY STREET
Northeast along Oldtown Mall and east from the 500 block of North Wolfe

A major east side road that starts at the edge of the downtown at Old Town Mall, and leaps housing projects and the Hopkins hospital to be reborn for about twenty blocks in the white-steps district of the east side. Tom McElderry, who lived 200 years ago, owned land under the present route. His claim to fame: he once loaned the city money to pave Baltimore Street.

McKIM STREET (AND AVENUE)
From the 700 block of East Madison Street north

The street is a short one just east of the Maryland State Penitentiary that recalls the name of an early-nineteenth-century family of merchant shipowners and philanthropists. The avenue is likewise short, a residential way in the Haddon Hall section near Bellona Avenue and Charles Street.

McMECHEN STREET
From the 1500 block of Pennsylvania Avenue northeast

An ancient street that cuts through the Bolton Hill district, McMechen is famed as the original home of the early sub-sandwich king, Harley Brinsfield. Brinsfield was also a jazz radio commentator and friend of blues all-timers like the Duke, Cab, Satchmo and Ella.

MELVIN AVENUE
From the 700 block of Fremont Avenue east

Lt. Norman E. Melvin, USAF, died over Germany in the 1940s, at age 20, while serving his country as a bombardier. This near west side street is named for him.

MERCER STREET
From the unit block of Light Street east

A glorified alley near ground zero of Baltimore, Mercer is named (most probably) for a 1790s worthy of the town, constable and innkeeper Benjamin James Mercer. His office and occupation doubtless meshed beautifully with the job of cooling off the boys. Today, appropriately, stylish pubs can be found along Mercer Street.

By the early 1970s, the ambitious, nineteen-acre Charles Center development had taken shape. It featured sleek architecture (at left) by Meis van der Rohe and the newly built Blaustein tower.

114

MERRYMAN LANE

It's a short one, an extension of busy University Parkway in Waverly. The namee was the family who built the surviving Clover Hill mansion, now the residence of Maryland's Episcopal bishop. The wealthy Virginia Merrymans (connections of the Duchess of Windsor) also apparently inspired Merryman Court, a Roland Park cul-de-sac, and Merryman's Mill Lane, an extension of Warren Road north of Loch Raven Reservoir. Still another Merryman's, a lane, leads south from the 700 block of Shawan Road. Most famous family member: John Merryman of Hayfields, locked up as a rebel sympathizer in 1861, and leading figure in the famous *Ex Parte Merryman* opinion on habeas corpus.

MOALE'S LANE (AND STREET)
From the 300 block of Greenspring Valley Road west

The John Moale family, early Baltimore settlers, owned Moale's Point at the end of the South Baltimore peninsula near Ferry Bar and the Hanover Street bridge. As late as the 1950s, short segments of Moale's Street survived on the point, but have since disappeared from modern maps. Moale's Lane exists as a short street in the lavish Greenspring Valley estate country north of town.

MONDAWMIN AVENUE
From the 2300 block of Monticello Road east

Mondawmin Mall is a major subway tourstop, but it's a good stroll from the mall westward to the avenue. It's an east-west street linking Walbrook and Windsor Hills. Mondawmin is an old Indian word for cornfield.

MONROE STREET
From the 2000 block of Whittier Avenue south

A major feeder for both Interstate 95 and the Baltimore Parkway south. Monroe Street on its lower stretches passes on one side of the road the city's oldest house (Mount Clare mansion) and on the other, what was once one of the largest retailing warehouses in the world, the Montgomery Ward building. The name comes from the nation's fifth president.

MONTGOMERY STREET
From Battery Avenue, Federal Hill, west

The most stylish street in the Federal Hill renewal area, with decks featuring glittery inner harbor skyline views, Montgomery has enriched original property owners (and the tax rolls) with incredible appreciations in value. The namesake was an early mayor. The street is historic because General Ben Butler marched up it to seize Baltimore at gunpoint in May of 1861. There's a Montgomery Road south of Reisterstown, and a Montgomery Court in the Catonsville Manor section of the western county.

MONUMENT STREET
From the 600 block of North Charles Street east and west

The east-west axis of Mount Vernon Square, Monument Street is one of America's noblest traditional spaces. Its east side perks with the small city bustle that is Johns Hopkins Hospital, its center with the song and sounds of the Peabody Conservatory. A little further west is No. 105, where Edwin Booth and Oscar Wilde, among other notables, often stopped when it was a nineteenth-century "private hotel." Also nearby is the Maryland Historical Society, with its unique collections of colonial portraits, silver, and early-nineteenth-century furniture.

MOORE STREET
From the 1900 block of West Baltimore Street
north and south

This one seems to have vanished in the construction of
King Boulevard, circling the west side. It was a one-
laner, paralleling surviving Orchard Street, and leading
off the 800 block of Madison Avenue. The namee was
David Moore, an early scientist-experimenter of the city.

MORAVIA ROAD
From the 4600 block of Belair Road southeast

Moravia defines the northern limits of Beverly Hills, a
small, well-preserved subdivision with some excellent
examples of the porch-and-shingle style of long ago. It
emerges from residential bliss and moves far to the
southwest, to be gobbled up in the roaring traffic boom
and spaghetti freeways of the Kennedy Highway.

MOSHER STREET
From the unit block of Malster Avenue off Mt.
Royal Avenue southwest

One of the best known east-west routes in the Bolton
Hill-Linden Avenue districts. Mosher Street was named
after a Boston transplant, a brickwork contractor who
helped to build the city's handsome Regency-style courthouse (long since vanished) of pre-Civil War years.

MOUNT HOLLY STREET
From the 3800 block of Bateman Avenue north

The Mount Holly Hotel, a humongous shingle appari-
tion that burned in a spectacular 1920s fire, was the most
famous feature of this west side street overlooking the
breezes of the Gwynns Falls Valley. The Mount Holly
name is older even than the hotel, built around 1900.

MOUNT ROYAL AVENUE (AND TERRACE)

From the 1400 block of North Charles Street
west

The eastern border of the Bolton Hill historical district, it features, on either side of a wide parkway, units of the Maryland Institute College of Art, the notable Baltimore & Ohio station, the 100-year-old Lyric Theater, and just a block away, Meyerhoff Hall, home of the city's symphony orchestra. In the horse and buggy days, the avenue and terrace to the north were a grand processional avenue to Druid Hill Park. Both still survive despite severe mauling during the building of the Jones Falls Expressway and the bomb-it-out renewal techniques of genius planners in the 1950s. The 1900 block of the terrace is one of the most impressive rows in American architecture of the Queen Anne school of urban design. At the terrace and Reservoir Street is a turn-of-the-century mansion where the pols cinched the nomination of Woodrow Wilson as the Democratic presidential contender.

NACIREMA LANE
North from Greenspring Valley Road just west
of Villa Julie College

Two unique personalities are associated with this road:
General Felix Agnus, the all-powerful nineteenth-
century editor of the *Baltimore American*, and the match-
less Met opera soprano, Rosa Ponselle. The general built
"Nacirema," a storied mansion in the finest Victorian
gargoyle style, on a Greenspring Valley hilltop. It was
replaced by Ponselle's surviving Latin villa, "Villa Pace,"
for three decades a center that fostered young vocal
artists under the diva's coaching.

NAPOLEON ALLEY
From the first block of South Eutaw Street west

A tiny lane on the west edge of the central business
district between Paca and Eutaw streets. Nobody seems
to know why the name is sometimes misspelled Na-
polean on some area maps.

NASHUA CIRCLE AND COURT
From the 3800 block of Coronado Place west

Baltimore loves to name streets after horses. The great
Nashua rates two, a cul-de-sac near Milford Mill High
School off Liberty Road, and a court off Kelso Drive
south of Rossville in Baltimore County.

NAUTILUS STREET
Three blocks north of Hammonds Lane just
west of Interstate 895

Nautilus pops up in an Anne Arundel county subdivision, Terrace View Estates. Everything here suggests
sunny vacations; streets are Surfside, Regatta, Sunset
Strip, and other cheery names. The light-hearted area is
located just west of Brooklyn Park.

N

119

NAYLOR'S LANE
From the 1700 block of Reisterstown Road,
Pikesville southwest to Old Court Road

One of the metro area's all-too-few escape routes,
known only to veteran drivers. This one offers a way of
dodging the massive tie-ups of Reisterstown Road at
Old Court Road en route to or from a local subway stop.
May their tribe increase.

NEW CUT ROADS
From the 12600 block of Harford Road
southeast

Surveying engineers and other folks dubbing streets
always have this title to fall back on when they're stuck
for a name, in case they can't even manage to work in
the name of a wife or a friend. One links Harford and
Belair roads out in Baltimore county near the Gunpowder River. In Anne Arundel County, it's an extension of
the Crain Highway, and in Howard County it leads out
of Ellicott City to connect with Montgomery Road on the
south.

NEW DEAL PLACE
Parallels Wise Avenue, Dundalk, along the 100 to
300 blocks

The name is a tribute, conscious or unconscious, to
President FDR, who coined the phrase for his administration. It parallels Wise Avenue in the Bear Creek area
north of Inverness.

NICHOLSON STREET
From the 1100 block of Hull Street southwest

A waterfront route in Locust Point named in honor of
Judge Joseph H. Nicholson, an early-nineteenth-century
patriot who took the manuscript of a poem written by
his wife's brother-in-law to a local printer. The poem was
"The Star-Spangled Banner."

NIMITZ DRIVE
The northwestern boundary of Fort McHenry, west from Wallace Street

The World War II Pacific admiral is remembered in this street bordering the Fort McHenry national monument.

NOBILITY COURT
Three blocks northeast of Reisterstown Road at Village Queen Drive

Another of many tributes to the good old days of castles and kings in the Queen Anne Village subdivision off Reisterstown Road.

NORMAL TERRACE (AND AVENUE)
From the first block of Burke Avenue, Towson, south

A short street off Burke Avenue in Towson, the name doesn't refer to serene residents, but probably to the fact that the state "normal" (teacher's) college was once nearby. The avenue is a short street leading east from Harford Road just south of Clifton Park.

NUNNERY LANE
From the 5800 block of Edmundson Avenue south

A two-block street north of Frederick Road near Baltimore National Cemetery. This part of the west end is known as Paradise. The street name dates well back in the nineteenth century. Nunnery was the access road to the covent-school of the nuns of the Order of the Visitation, now the Mount de Sales Academy, an all-girl high school.

O'DONNELL STREET
From the 1000 block of Lakewood Avenue east

Today a showcase of waterfront renewal, O'Donnell Street is a parkway with a center island big enough for churches and branch libraries, a place that still preserves village charm, just north of the burgeoning swank of north harbor condos. In the middle of it all is a fine statue of John O'Donnell, the eighteenth-century China Sea trader who started the Canton area along the road from sailing-era hub to oil and metal manufacturing center. Its present horizon seems to be developing into a sort of Maryland version of Fort Lauderdale.

OLIVER STREET (S)
From the 1500 block of Guilford Avenue east
and 1500 Charles west

There's a short block with this name in the Mt. Washington shopping center, but the real thing starts downtown. Few city streets are chopped into weirder segments than Oliver, named for a merchant moneybags of the early nineteenth century. It starts near the Maryland Institute in Mount Royal, jumps the Jones Falls to reappear and then disappear at Greenmount Avenue, only to be reborn on the other side of the Greenmount Cemetery. It vanishes at Edison Highway, and has still more incarnations, one in Armistead Gardens, and another even further west in Rosedale, south of Philadelphia Road.

OLMSTEAD ROAD AND AVENUE
From the 1000 block of Kingston Road south

The Olmsted family of architects, planners, and landscape geniuses is responsible for these without a doubt misspelled local streets. Olmstead Road is in the Sudbrook Park planned community, which members of the family had a hand in, and Olmstead Street is in the Curtis Bay area. Olmstead Green is a street in the 1960s center city planned town of Cross Keys.

OTTERBEIN STREET
From the 700 block of Carroll Street north

Old Otterbein Church, built in 1785, still stands near the harbor and in the glitzy middle of the city's new hotel district, but the family's street memorial is about three-quarters of a mile due west, just behind King Boulevard. It comes in two short segments in the Washington Village restoration area. The name honors United Brethren Bishop Philip W. Otterbein, who emigrated to America from Germany in 1774, and was one of the church's early bishops.

PACA STREET
From the 500 block of West Baltimore Street
north and south

There's some doubt as to whether or not William Paca, an illustrious signer of the Declaration of Independence, was Italian, but there's no mystery at all about his namesake street in downtown Baltimore. Paca Street moves resolutely northbound from the Russell Street extension of the Baltimore-Washington Parkway until it suddenly expires just short of the State Office Center in Mount Royal. Major sights along the way include the University of Maryland Medical Center, the Lexington Market, and the restored district of Seton Hill. Nobody who drives in downtown Baltimore can miss hitting Paca at some point; hardly anybody knows there's another Paca Street paralleling the railroad tracks as they cross Hollins Ferry Road.

PADONIA ROAD
From Lake Circle east of Pot Springs Road west
to Falls Road

One of the main players in the vast expansion of north central Baltimore County, Padonia begins in the blissful, expensive club land about five miles north of town, and runs almost to the Loch Raven Reservoir on the east. On the way it catches a vast variety of lifestyles, from horsey estates to balconied apartments to shopping centers.

PARK HEIGHTS AVENUE
From the 3400 block of Reisterstown Road
northwest

Some of the best and some of the very worst city environments show their colors along the seven or so miles of this major artery on the northwest side. The lower stretches, built in the early twentieth century for blue collar and middle-income types, has deteriorated rapidly despite heroic efforts, and can compete with

Paca Street recalls William Paca, probably the first Italian-born governor of an American state.

Pennsylvania Avenue, cradle of Baltimore jazz and swing greats, housed the famous Royal Theater of the black entertainment circuit. The Royal, near this stretch of road, succumbed to renewal clearance of the area between Mt. Royal and Reservoir Hill.

other impacted eastern urban centers that have decayed. The upper stretches, where deluxe apartment living slowly gives way to superb custom subdivisions, and in turn, to magnificent estates, are among the state's highest income areas. The change from marginal living to Shangri-La is abrupt.

PARK AVENUE
From the 600 block of Whitelock Street south

One of the most nostalgic and colorful of luxury horse-and-buggy townhouse streets. F. Scott Fitzgerald, author of *The Great Gatsby,* lived for a while at No. 1307. He gazed out the window at a monument on Eutaw Place to his relative, Francis Scott Key. Park Avenues also haunt Towson, Halethorpe, and Essex.

PARNELL AVENUE
Just inside the city line west of Ralls Avenue

The street runs off Central Avenue in the St. Helena section of Dundalk. The Bureau of Surveys named it Parnell because it fit into an alphabetical listing scheme. But Irish tradition, begorra, now says it honors the martyred Irish nationalist, Charles Stewart Parnell.

PATTERSON AVENUE
From the 6500 block of Liberty Road northeast

Though the Patterson name became almost holy in Baltimore, there were those in the family who did not care for the city. One was Betsy, daughter of William, the Irish-American millionaire (see Patterson Park Avenue). Betsy was married to Jerome Bonaparte, the French dictator's brother, for a time (until Nappy annulled the marriage, despite the fact that they had children), and she lived for a time in Europe. One November night in London she wrote, "In my dreams I am transported to the populous desert of Baltimore and awake shuddering." She would probably not shudder today if she could see this street. As a canny real estate investor who lived to a great age, she might admire it. From Liberty Road to beneath the elevated section of the Baltimore subway, Patterson Avenue is a leafy parade of attractive small homes—Cape Cods, Dutch Colonials, and such—and overhead is one of the finer stands of mature hardwoods in the city limits.

PATTERSON PARK AVENUE
From the 2300 block of East Baltimore Street north and south

This street moves down the east side's white-steps district and the stained-glass-window neighborhoods until it almost reaches the harbor, defining the east side of the park in a series of descending row homes that include some of the eastern section's most solid and interesting Victorian structures. The park name honors William Patterson, the American Revolution blockade runner who later became one of the pillars of Maryland commerce. He lived on the park site.

July 1902: A furious tornado ripped through the Patterson Park highlands. It wrecked this building and 300 to 400 others in just a few minutes.

PAYSON STREET AND AVENUE
From the 2000 block of West Baltimore Street north and south

Payson hops, skips, and even jumps through the city's west side, moving due south from near Mondawmin Mall to join up with the lower stretches of Monroe Street. The avenue is a short block near Catonsville Center. Henry Payson, typical of so many Baltimore pioneers, was a New Englander. He helped plan Battle Monument and founded the First Unitarian Church.

127

PEABODY COURT AND MEWS
Two blocks northwest of Harford Road at Harford Village Drive

George Peabody was a brilliant international banker from New England, who befriended Baltimore and Nashville with educational largesse by creating the Peabody Institute in the middle of the last century. There's a short street in Carney with his name, and also a mews, a one-time alley, paralleling Mount Vernon Place behind the conservatory he founded.

PEARCE AVENUE
From the 3400 block of Taney Road northwest

A bunch of nineteenth-century Maryland worthies are remembered in subdivision streets south of Cross Country Boulevard in the extreme northwestern corner of Baltimore. James Alfred Pearce was a Civil War-era senator who opposed both coercing the South and the Lincoln administration's policy of locking up his political pals.

PEN LUCY ROAD AND AVENUE
Three blocks north over Wickham Road from Frederick Avenue

Pen Lucy was a boys' school organized by nineteenth-century southern author and Georgian emigrant, Richard Malcolm Johnston. Two streets bear the name of the long-ago-expired school; the original avenue in Waverly, and the road in the west side's Irvington section.

128

PERINE COURT, LANE AND PLACE
One block southeast of the 10000 block of Harford Road

Way out in Cub Hill where they clog to bluegrass on Harford Road is this cluster of names. The Perines, Baltimore bluebloods of the first water, would not be amused. Or would they?

PERRY ROAD
One block east of the 4600 block of Ridge Road southwest off Fitch Avenue

There was a Perry Street downtown west of South Charles Street that seems to have disappeared under inner harbor renewal, but all is not lost—there's a Perry Road. It perhaps unconsciously revives a street name that honored Commodore O.H.P. Perry, who fought the Battle of Lake Erie in September of 1813. The road is in Fullerton.

PHILADELPHIA ROAD AND ROUTES

Belair Road becomes one of the old Philly routes at the city line, and seems to go on forever as U.S. 1. It's an interesting, old-timey way of reaching the mushroom country across the state line and the Wilmington-Philadelphia region. The old Philadelphia Road eventually gets there too, but with less scenery.

PHILPOT STREET AND ROAD
A dead end street reached by crossing Dock or Thames Street on the Allied Chemical Plant peninsula

The street's a waterfront block in Fells Point, the road a rural route at Phoenix north of Hunt Valley in Baltimore County. The namee for the street was Brian Philpot, Jr., an English emigrant who played a significant role in town affairs during Baltimore's earliest years, before the boom of the late eighteenth century.

129

POOLE STREET
From the 1300 block of West 36th Street south

Robert Poole, an Irish foundryman and ironmaster, cast the iron capitals for the U. S. Capitol building and the Treasury at his Woodberry plant. He's remembered today in the plant area with Poole Street, which borders Roosevelt Park and the Robert Poole Middle School, not far away.

The 123-foot dome of the Mount Clare shops of the Baltimore & Ohio Railroad Museum towers over the station, the oldest passenger ticket office in the world.

POPPLETON STREET
From the 900 block of Washington Boulevard north

It moves north from busy, east-bound Pratt Street on the near west side of town. Nicely restored, workaday row houses of two and three stories, some 150 years old, now mark the area, with a minipark or two. The star of the show is the magnificent, relic-stuffed Baltimore & Ohio Railroad Museum, graciously endowed by the Chessie System to the tune of $5 million. The museum's enormous "roundhouse," topped by a 123-foot cupola, is one of the greatest specimens of 1880s industrial architecture. Thomas Poppleton was an early-nineteenth-century surveyor. The street appears with his name on it on a map the surveyor prepared in 1822.

PORTER STREET AND PORTER'S LANE
Two blocks northeast of Martin Boulevard at Windlass Road

David Porter was a hell-for-leather sea captain who fought the British in the War of 1812. As recently as the 1950s a street named in his honor was identified and in business near Federal Hill. It appears to have disappeared. However, there is still a Porter's Lane near Martin Plaza in the Victory Villa section of eastern Baltimore County.

POTEE STREET
From the Hanover Street bridge to Route 2 (Ritchie Highway) at the city line

Potee is the southbound lane of the Ritchie Highway connector from the Hanover Street bridge into Brooklyn. John E. Potee was one of the most popular Baltimore politicos of the early twentieth century, sheriff of the city and Democratic stalwart of stalwarts.

131

POTHOUSE ALLEY
Southeast of the 200 block of Gay Street

It's a lane paralleling Gay Street in the heart of the "Old Town" district, ancient ward of theatrical folk, cut-purses, and other riff-raff. Just a few blocks to the southeast was the townhouse of the most famous of Baltimore thespians, the Booths, who lived in a row house on North Exeter Street. The Booth boys put up a stage in the backyard at an early age for the performance of amateur theatricals. John Wilkes, it is said, always played the maidenly heroine.

POTOMAC STREET
From the 3000 block of Federal Street south

It starts on the heights just below Baltimore Cemetery on the old east side and bounds southward all the way to the harbor, taking time out to leap St. Alphonsus churchyard, Bocek Park, Pulaski Highway, and Patterson Park.

PRATT STREET
From the 200 block of South Charles Street
east and west

This central harbor artery takes eastbound traffic from points west, along a parade of highrises and the margins of "Little Italy," and onward to the vast reaches and white steps of the east side. It's the tragedy and triumph street of the city. The tragedy came in April 1861 when the Civil War shooting first started. Civilians took pot-shots at Massachusetts militia trying to reach Camden railroad station for a trip south. The triumph is what good planning has achieved. Pratt is the showcase of a grand artery featuring the National Aquarium, a World Trade Center, a Fortune 500 highrise, the highest earning shopping center (per square foot) in the nation, and a dock for the hoary U.S.S. *Constellation*, dating from 1797, said to be the oldest warship afloat.

A highly imaginary version of the famous 6th Masschusetts riots on
April 19, 1861.

The morass of West Pratt Street traffic about 1906.

PRESSTMAN STREET
From the 1500 block of Hilton Street east

This street runs through the west side south of North Avenue. It was originally supposed to honor one George Presstman, a founder of the First Baptist Church of Baltimore, but the city never opened the street he had dedicated. "Why not name it after Judge Ben Presstman," said a city father in 1866, when they finally got ready to cut the street through—forty-seven years after the death of George. The deed was done, though Judge Presstman was no relation of the earlier man. George was unlucky in real estate, too. He and his Baptist elders sank $50,000 into the first church's magnificent Roman-temple style building, designed by Robert Mills, and it took two generations to pay off the debt.

Curious Lore

Loudon Park Cemetery was once a popular tourist spot. Trolley tracks were laid through it so that the curious could travel in comfort.

PULASKI HIGHWAY AND STREET
Northeast and southwest from 63rd Street at the city line and from the 2100 block of West Baltimore Street north and south

Casimir Pulaski, the Polish patriot, has plenty of memorials in Baltimore. One is the big east side highway (U. S. 40 north), one of the granddaddy's of national truck travel. The street parallels Payson Street on the west side, and continues south with a few breaks to Wilkens Avenue.

PURNELL DRIVE
From the 5800 block of Gwynn Oak Avenue
south

Purnell Drive connects Gwynn Oak Avenue with Forest
Park Avenue, winding through Hillsdale Park. L. Bowen
Purnell was an Eastern shoreman who came to Baltimore in the 1850s and married into the wealthy Hurst
dry goods family.

QUAD AVENUE
From the 700 block of North Point Boulevard
northeast and southwest

A recently developed industrial district has Quad Avenue as a main stem. It lies just north of Canton Industrial Park on both sides of the city line.

QUARTERFIELD ROAD
Northeast and southwest from Route 3 south
of Dorsey Road

Once a rather quiet road linking Glen Burnie with the Ridgeway-Odenton area to the southwest in Anne Arundel County. Quarterfield became a major throughway with the completion of Route 100, which it crosses, and the development of the Old Mill residential area and points further south in the county.

QUEEN ANNE ROAD AND STREET
Northeast from Old Annapolis Road at the
Arundel expressway

About half the streets that begin with the letter Q in the Baltimore region are some sort of version of Queen Anne, an unhappy queen who had little or nothing to do with Maryland in the early eighteenth century. Queen Anne is a road off the old Annapolis road in Harundale, a road again in Windsor Hills, again in Westview, and yet again off Taylor Avenue near Parkville. There's also a Queen's Ferry Road, a major drive in the Glenmont section east of Towson, and a Queen's Road a few blocks east of North Arundel General Hospital. With nine streets named after queens, Anne Arundel ranks as easily the most royally oriented of area counties. For a woman who may never have heard of Maryland colony, let alone the yet-to-be-conceived Baltimore, Anne's name may be a little overused.

QUENTIN ROAD
From the 1800 block of East Joppa Road
southeast

There are two of these, one off Joppa Road in Baynes-
ville, and another in the Inverness section of Dundalk.
Speculation indicates that there is a 50–50 chance the
roads were named after 1) somebody named Quentin,
2) the famous battlefield in France during World War I in
which Maryland men in uniform were engaged.

Curious Lore

Maryland's first drive-in movie theatre opened for summer shows in the
early 1900s at 36th Street and Roland Avenue, Hampden.

QUIMPER COURT
Two blocks northwest of the 4300 block of Old
Court Road

The deluxe Brittany apartment community off the Beltway at Pikesville used French provincial names for its
streets when it opened several decades ago. Quimper is
the traditional (and expensive) peasant pottery of the
western French province of the same name, bordered by
the English Channel and the Atlantic.

R

RADECKE AVENUE
From the 4900 block of Frankford Avenue
northeast

This is an important crosstown street on the far east side of town, linking Rosedale with closer-in places like Gardenville and Cedonia. Dietrich Radecke was a Hanoverian German born in Napoleon's time. He learned the wheelwright's trade, came to the U.S. in his early twenties, and landed with eight dollars in his pocket. He soon prospered as a box factory executive, and after the Civil War bought a sixty-eight-acre farm, Gardenville, off Belair Road. The old farm road that is now Radecke Avenue was named for him.

RAMSAY STREET
From the 300 block of South Fulton Avenue
east and west

It starts at Bentalou Street on the old southwest side, and moves due east to vanish at the main line of the B&O railroad, only to reappear in Washington Village, not far from the harbor and the central business district. Col. Nathaniel Ramsay was a Maryland attack officer in the Continental Army. His commander, George, when president, named him commander of the Baltimore naval district.

Nathaniel Ramsey, a Washington lieutenant, saved the day after the Revolutionary rout at the battle of Monmouth.

RASPE AVENUE
From the 6100 block of Walther Avenue
southeast

A sleepy, leafy old place named Raspeburg, that disappeared into Belair Road developments long ago, was named for local storekeeper, John Henry Raspe. In turn, Raspe Avenue got its name from the village and the village from Raspe, a Union Army civil war vet. Today Raspe is in four pieces, from Hamilton Street to Overlea.

RAYLEIGH WAY
From the 6300 block of Toone Street north

A short street in the O'Donnell Heights development in East Baltimore, Rayleigh honors John William Strutt, Lord Rayleigh, a Nobel prize-winning scientist.

RAYNER AVENUE
From the 700 block of North Payson Street west

It's another stop-and-start street in the southern part of the Harlem Park area. William S. Rayner was an 1840 immigrant to the U.S. who helped found the Locust Point industrial development area. His son was a Maryland senator.

REDWOOD STREET
From the unit block of Light Street east and west

Stately Redwood, though not quite as illustrious as it once was, rated as the city's Wall Street under the name German Street. When America entered the fray against the "Huns" in 1917, intense propoganda made German a dirty word. The midtown artery was changed to Redwood, named after Lt. George B. Redwood, a newspaperman who enlisted in the intelligence corps and was killed in Northern France.

REGESTER AVENUE
From the 1700 block of Orleans Street north and south

Three major suburban subdivisions, Rodgers Forge, Stoneleigh, and Idlewylde, are linked by this important and interesting mid-twentieth-century street with its varied architecture and housing approaches. Joshua

Regester, who deeded much of the route to Baltimore County, was a successful foundry president. There's also a Regester Street in Fells Point, and a second street paralleling Broadway near North Avenue. They are named for various family members.

REISTERSTOWN ROAD
From the 1600 block of West North Avenue north

This is the road alignment that fed nineteenth century Baltimore, that echoed with the rumble of grain and flour wagons for a century. To the south it becomes Pennsylvania Avenue; to the north, the main stem for busy Pimlico and Pikesville until it passes swanky Garrison and Owings Mills. North of Reisterstown the route becomes the Hanover Pike (State Route 30) linking increasingly gentrified towns like Manchester and Hampstead. Gourmet dining, major private schools, upscale shopping and deluxe townhouse and garden apartment communities are among the attractions.

RELLIM ROAD
From the 6000 block of Greenspring Avenue west and north

A short suburban street in a choice residential district, Rellim Road is named for Hal A. Miller, a native of Canada and a functionalist architect of the 1950s. Miller died at age forty-nine, but his name lives forever, even if it is spelled backwards. The street connects with Greenspring Avenue.

REMINGTON AVENUE
From the 200 block of West 27th Street north

The main stem of the shirtsleeve Remington neighborhood, boxed in between the Falls, Wyman Park, and 25th Street. It used to be a haven for car sales agencies.

Its most going operation is the taxicab business directed from Sisson Street nearby.

REMLEY STREET
From the 1700 block of Chesapeake Avenue north

In industrial Fairfield, the street is a memorial, probably the only one, to Harry Remley. He was appointed to the "Commission for Opening Streets" in 1913 as a total political unknown. When Harry died in 1924 he was commission chairman and the survivors named this street in his honor.

RESERVOIR STREET
Fom the 2000 block of Mt. Royal Terrace west

A short, 1890s street that dead ends at Mount Royal Terrace, Reservoir still boasts the old Bond mansion (vastly converted to different uses) called "Mount Royal," and some distinctive home restorations. Hugh Lennox Bond of Mount Royal worked tirelessly to improve black schools, and as a judge won equal rights for black soldiers in the Civil War pay lines. The racially integrated blocks of Reservoir serve as a reminder of Bond's lifelong mission to help others.

REVERDY STREET
Southeast from Northern Parkway two blocks north of Belvedere Avenue

This residential street runs east and west in Govans, just west of Chinquapin Parkway. Reverdy Johnson, Jr., the street's godfather, was the wealthy son of a greater father, Reverdy Sr., a Civil War loyalist and great constitutional lawyer. Johnson quit the Lincoln conspiracy trials because he thought defendants were being railroaded by military law. Modern historians are not so sure.

Dr. Thomas Bond, lord of the "Mount Royal" estate in Reservoir Hill that gave its name to the district.

RICKENBACKER ROAD
Two blocks southwest of the 1700 block of Eastern Boulevard

Rickenbacker is a looped street in the Mars estates subdivision off Eastern Boulevard. Eddie Rickenbacker was an all-timer of U.S. aviation who warmed up to his career on racing cars. He went on to become a World War I ace, national speed recordholder, and wartime aide to the Defense Department in World War II.

RIDGELY ROAD, STREET, AND AVENUE
East and west of York Road at York Ridge Shopping Center

The road connects the York and Dulaney Valley roads through a splendid residential area. The Ridgelys were one of the FFM (First Families of Maryland), who owned nearby "Hampton," now a national monument. Charles Ridgely of Hampton was a two-term state governor. The Ridgely Street in Mount Winans is believed to have been named for him. There is a Ridgely Avenue in Thornwood Park off East Joppa Road.

RINGGOLD STREET
From the 700 block of Ramsay Street north

Residents of tiny Ringgold Street will soon be able to walk to the ballpark after the Camden area stadium is finished. Sam Ringgold was an important artillerist who died at the battle of Palo Alto in the Mexican War.

RITTENHOUSE AVENUE
From the 3300 block of Washington Boulevard north

A suburban street that appears in Lansdowne off Washington Boulevard and reappears about a mile east inside the city line in the Lakeland section. James Rittenhouse, a descendant of the famed Philadelphia family, was a powerful Democratic overlord in the southwestern county. He was also instrumental in founding the Halethorpe community.

ROGERS AVENUE
From the 1400 block of Northern Parkway north and west

A major route in the city's northwestern area, running all the way from the Jones Falls in center city to Liberty Road, far out on the northwest side. It is a major border of the Pimlico district. Edmund Law Rogers was superintendent of the Maryland Jockey Club when it all started, Oct. 25, 1870, when an almost unknown horse named Preakness won the Dinner Party Stakes.

ROLAND AVENUE
From the 700 block of West Lake Avenue south

The main stem of Baltimore's unchanging preppyville, which is a north end settlement built up in the 1890s and 1900s. The area was the scene of Anne Tyler's prose epics, and a movie derived therefrom. As a museum of Queen Anne shingle-and-porch architectural fancies, and turn-of-the-century stained glass whimsy, it has few rivals in U.S. cities. Private schools, Volvos, Mercs, BMWs and Jags are all at curbside.

RUSCOMBE LANE
From the 4800 block of Lanier Avenue north

The street runs east and west just east of the Pimlico elementary school, and is named for the Greenspring Avenue estate of "Ruscombe."

RUSSELL STREET
From the King Boulevard overpass at Hamburg Street south

No one can miss this major artery. It drives through the southwestern industry of the city, headed straight for the city's skyline. Alexander Russell, an Irishman who came to America in 1781, inspired the name. He was a brick manufacturer who prospered mightily, in more ways than one—he was the father of twenty kids.

RUTTER STREET
From the unit block of Mosher Street south

A much-admired rainbow block of tiny homes behind the Maryland Institute's Genoese palace on Mt. Royal Avenue. The name comes from an old Jones Falls ford.

SABINA AVENUE
One block north of the 1100 block of Northern Parkway via Mattfeldt Avenue

A residential street in lower Mt. Washington named for the daughter-in-law of the original neighborhood resident (see Mattfeldt Avenue). It's pronounced Sa-bee-na.

ST. PAUL STREET
From the 4300 block of North Charles Street south

A ride through city history that has a grand finale, St. Paul starts in the midtown residential enclave of Guilford where 1920s wealth built Tudor castles, Georgian halls, and French chateaus. It escapes into more seriously intellectual Homewood, stretching with some decorum past a hospital complex and rows of architectural monuments, at least two the work of famed New York architects, McKim, Meade and White. Church steeples punctuate the route getting older and older

Not London, but Baltimore's lawyer-haunted "old court" district in the midtown area. These buildings, including the handsome Maryland Historical Society palace (at far left) were bulldozed over in the creation of Preston Gardens and St. Paul Place.

145

St. Paul Place and St. Paul Street at Preston Gardens, the city's most lasting "city beautiful" improvements, after the Orleans Street overpass (in distance) had been finished. The city's first parking building (left center) is on the corner of Saratoga Street.

while the row homes get more impressive toward center city. At Centre Street, St. Paul commits binary fission, dividing into two one-way streets; an upper drive, St. Paul Place, lined with highrises, and a lower one off Preston Gardens that is fearsome to cross on foot. St. Paul abruptly disappears in front of the city's magnificent court building and becomes Light Street. (The court building has been used by Hollywood as the setting for a number of "trial" movies.) It's quite a ride.

ST. VICTOR STREET
From the 900 block of Patapsco Avenue south

The street is in the heart of Brooklyn, south of Patapsco Avenue. It recalls Saint Victor I, an early pope. Nearby is Saint Margaret Street, named for Saint Margaret of Cortona. Developer-builder Victor Frenkil, Sr., named both streets after his son, Victor, Jr., recovered from a devastating accident at the age of three. His wife, who naturally suffered through the injury of her son, was named Margaret, hence the addition of that street name.

SAN MARTIN DRIVE
From the 100 block of West University Parkway south

This heavily treed, winding affair is situated on the western border of the Johns Hopkins University campus. Jose San Martin, the George Washington of the southern South American states, is honored.

SARATOGA STREET
From the 300 block of North Charles Street east and west

One of the hoariest of city streets, Saratoga is the northern border of Charles Center, the 1960s and 1970s office renewal project of nineteen acres of highrises, plazas, and a theater. Saratoga features center city's steepest hill. It moves on westward to terminate in an elementary school. Two short segments of the street also survive east and west of Hilton Street. The Revolution's Battle of Saratoga is remembered here.

The city's narrowest street, Rock Street, off West Saratoga, was bulldozed over, all six feet of its width.

SCHLEY AVENUE
From the 3900 block of Southern Avenue southwest

A Gardenville street in the northeastern suburbs remembers Admiral Winfield Scott Schley, a Frederick (Md.) native whose role in the Battle of Santiago during the Spanish-American War became a notorious cause celebré.

SCHROEDER STREET
From the 900 block of Harlem Avenue south

The Schroeders were a German family of the west side whose Greek Revival mansion was one of the showplaces of the horse and buggy era. There's an avenue of this name out on Belair road in the Fullerton Farms development. The main event, a long north-south street, runs from Harlem Avenue to West Pratt Street.

SCHWARTZ AVENUE
From the 6300 block of York Road northwest

Also spelled Schwarz, this street recalls a toy store owner of German background who settled in Baltimore in 1860. Henry Schwarz was the local Santa Claus who ran the place; his brothers helped out, then opened up their own shops, including the world-famous F.A.O. Schwartz establishment in Manhattan. The street is in the Pinehurst section just east of York Road over the city line. Local Schwartz Park is also in memory of the family.

SCOTT STREET
From the 700 block of Ostend Street southeast and northwest

Scott is a little-known, but long route that runs all the way from West Lombard Street to the heart of industrial Camden. It was named for Winfield Scott, a military genius of the rank of Grant, Lee, and Sherman. This memorial is not for the general's smashing of the Mexican army in the 1840s, but for his performance for the nation in the War of 1812. He was just thirty years old when given this honor; except for war heroes killed in action, possibly a record for male recipients of street name honors.

SEMINARY AVENUE
From the 1400 block of Providence Road west

A fine, suburban ramble of about six miles that runs from Providence Road on the east to Falls Road on the west. It passes a deluxe housing region, a Carmelite monastery, leafy Victorian Lutherville, the battlements of old Maryland College for Women (now a health care center), vaults the roar of the Baltimore-Harrisburg Expressway, and terminates westward at the gate of St. Paul's School for Girls.

SENKER PLACE
From the 2300 block of Pennsylvania Avenue northeast

Sam Senker's dray horse had been on the job so long delivering rugs and upholstered furniture for the Senkers' company that he knew all the stops without signals. The place, which remembers Sam, if not the horse, is a glorified alley that takes off at a forty-five-degree angle from Pennsylvania Avenue to link up with West North Avenue.

SEVERSKY COURT
From the 1700 block of Eastern Boulevard southeast

A genial Russian who lost a leg in World War I, Seversky was recruited by the U.S. as a consulting aeronautical engineer, and decorated by President Truman. His street appears in the Mars Estates neighborhood south and north of Eastern Boulevard, where a rash of aerial greats are remembered in street signs.

SEWER ROAD
From Exit 39 of Interstate 695 east

Don't get excited. It's not anywhere near your neighborhood, but part of the Back River sewage disposal plant.

SHAKESPEARE STREET
From the 800 block of South Broadway west

It's one of the more historic and pricey of the Fells Point restoration routes along the 200-year-old stretches of the north harbor. It leads (one way, please) off festive Market Place. The bard would probably be pleased. Locals have had since 1796 to come see the sign.

SHARP STREET
From the 100 block of West Conway Street east and west

Old timers spelled this route the same way the colonial Governor, Horatio Sharpe, spelled it when the street was named for the family. It leads from the west side of the federal court house on Lombard Street southward to Henrietta Street.

SHAWAN ROAD
From Exit 20 of Interstate 83 east and west

A once-bucolic north Baltimore County route that now forms the main spine of the Hunt Valley business center development.

SHIRLEY AVENUE
From the 3900 block of Reisterstown Road northeast

Not many Victorian gentlemen emigrated to Maryland from England. One who did was William Shirley, whose ancestors were china and glass merchants. William possessed his family's talents, and also founded a successful artware firm. Today's Shirley Avenue was once a lane leading to his country estate, northeast of Druid Hill Park.

SIMMS AVENUE
From the 4000 block of Southern Avenue southwest

The admiral, William Snowden, spelled it with one *m*, but the street named for him uses two. Somebody in the office wasn't paying attention. It's just north of Belair Road in Gardenville. Sims was a born whistle-blower who attempted to scrape the barnacles off entrenched U.S. Navy traditions.

SINCLAIR LANE
From the 1900 block of Belair Road east

It's a major convenience road that links the 25th Street industrial area in center city with the Frankford-Moravia area near the eastern city line.

SIPPLE AVENUE
From the 4800 block of Frankford Avenue southwest

Louis Sipple was a German immigrant's son who went into farming. One day, he simply put up a street sign with his name on it at the entrance to his property. When the city surveyors showed up, they left it that way. The street is in two pieces; one between Overlea and Fullerton, apparently the original, and another closer to downtown, running from Frankford Avenue to Moravia Road.

SISSON STREET
From the 2900 block of Wyman Park Drive south

An important service and light industry street between Wyman Park Drive and 25th Street known for many years as the headquarters for the city's waning taxi service. Hugh Sisson was the nineteenth-century marble king of Baltimore.

SLINGLUFF AVENUE
From the 2700 block of Baker Street south

When last seen, only about 150 feet of this once-prominent west side street was left. The WPA projects of the 1930s renamed most of it. The Slingluffs were wealthy gentry who equipped the Second Maryland Cavalry in the Civil War, and lived at "Beech Hill," a west side estate in what today is the Walbrook section. This is proof that a street can just slowly die.

SMALLWOOD STREET
From 2200 West Baltimore Street south and north

This one starts at the Mount Clare yards west of center city and heads north, leaping a major railroad yard and ending at Frederick Douglass High School north of North Avenue. William Smallwood was a portly Maryland revolutionary colonel, who had been educated at Eton in England, and a pal of George Washington.

SMITH AVENUE
From 5800 Falls Road west

It is hard to visualize the north end's Mount Washington community without Smith Avenue, a main axial route for the historic, treed district. The Smiths were from Yorkshire, farm folk who ended up running one of the city's florishing dry goods businesses.

STANSBURY LANE
One block west of the 300 block of Back River Neck Road off Browns Road

The Stansburys were probably the most famous east Baltimore county family of the nineteenth century. Elijah was a mayor of the city. There's a Stansbury Road in Dundalk, and a Stansbury Mill Road in the Sweet Air section of Baltimore County.

STERRETT STREET
From the 700 block of West Cross Street north

This street runs south of West Pratt Street and into southwest Baltimore. The main associations come from the Sterrett family's connection with the British invasion of 1814, when males of the clan turned out to get whipped at Bladensburg and then to taste triumph at North Point. Col. Joseph Sterrett was the most famous family member, a merchant and auctioneer.

STEVENSON LANE (AND ROAD)
From 6200 North Charles Street east

The lane runs north from upper Charles Street through the Rodgers Forge and Stoneleigh communities, then turns north to end in east Towson. The road starts in Pikesville, moves north through luxury subdivisions, a boutique shopping center at the village of Stevenson, and finally expires in Greenspring Valley.

STILES STREET
From the 1100 block of Gough Street west

An ancient one that begins at the waterline at Falls Avenue in the north harbor, it runs five blocks to seedy Central Avenue. Capt. George Stiles was a hawkish, anti-British "marine artillerist" in 1814, riddling British schooners with shot. In 1817, after the war, he created an experimental steamboat that made a two-mile trip in the harbor.

Curious Lore

In 1969 a home seven feet, three inches wide was identified in St. Mary's Street, Seton Hill.

STIRLING STREET
From the 1100 block of East Monument Street south

Lower Stirling Street near the Old Town mall is a remarkable restoration of an 1830s working man's quarter. The north end of Stirling runs from Madison to Aisquith Street. It was probably named for the Stirling family, distinguished Scotch immigrants who became wealthy importing merchants. They owned land in the area, and a summer estate, around 1800.

153

STOCKTON STREET
From the 1200 block of West Lexington Street south

It's one of the city's copious tributes to founding fathers. Richard Stockton, of New Jersey, was a "Signer" (of the Declaration of Independence). The route is on the near west side of town, between Franklin, Mulberry's freeway, and West Pratt Street.

STOKES DRIVE
From the 1300 block of Wildwood Parkway east and west

Dr. William Royal Stokes is one of two medical researchers remembered in city street names (see Lazear Street). His nemesis was the dreaded parrot's disease (psittacosis). Stokes Drive is a southern boundary of the Gwynns Falls Park.

STOLL STREET
From the 900 block of 10th Street west

It's a three-blocker in the middle of Brooklyn. It remembers the Stoll family, 1860 immigrants from Germany who went into the vegetable business near the street site. They stayed on to take up leading roles in the south Baltimore community when Brooklyn was engulfed with new homeowners.

STRICKER STREET
From the 1500 block of West Baltimore Street north and south

John Stricker may have been Maryland's most talented general of the early Republican period. He fought the battle of North Point that drove the redcoats back. His street is one of the dozens that thread north and south through the west side, forming the west side of Franklin Square and just missing the west side of Union Square.

SULGRAVE AVENUE
From the 5700 block of Greenspring Avenue
east

This street was christened in 1927. It is customary to link it to Sulgrave Manor, ancestral home of the Washingtons in England. It bisects both Pimlico and Mount Washington.

SUMMIT AVENUE
One block north of the 1400 block of Frederick
Road

There are at least six Summit Avenues in the immediate Baltimore area, and five Summits in Anne Arundel County, but the one with the oldest history is in the heart of Catonsville. This Summit Avenue remembers Gen. James A. Gary, onetime postmaster general of the U.S., a Republican leader, and onetime owner of the Alberton Mills at Daniels, Howard County. "Summit" was his estate in Catonsville, and the street borders its site.

SZOLD DRIVE
From the 3100 block of Bonnie Road north

Near the city line in the northwestern residential district of Fallstaff, this street recalls Henrietta Szold. Szold, a pioneering Jewish intellectual at the turn of the century, devoted her mature years to international affairs, including the welfare programs of the Hadassah. The Zionist spokeswoman revolutionized middle-eastern health and hygiene conditions.

T

TANEY ROAD
From the 6000 block of Wallis Avenue north and south

This residential street cuts through the Cheswolde area near the western run in northwest Baltimore. It is named for Roger Brooke Taney, onetime chief justice of the nation. His Dred Scott decision, that slaves remained property of owners even in free states, helped fuel the murderous passions of the Civil War.

TAZEWELL ROAD
From the 2000 block of Wetheredsville Road west

Virginia names abound in the west Baltimore community of Windsor Hills. This one appears to be named after one of the famed Old Dominion clans who intermarried with Maryland gentry in the old days.

TESSIER COURT
From the 500 block of St. Mary Street northwest

A short street near the old St. Mary's seminary property on the near northwest side, it is one of the only remnants of the French presence in the Seton Hill district. Father Jean Marie Tessier, a refugee from the French Revolution, and other Sulpician clerics founded St. Mary's in the city in July 1791.

TEXAS LANDFILL ROAD
From the 10400 block of York Road west

Not a tribute to the Lone Star State, podner, but the old Texas quarry country north of the city. It now forms one of the southern borders of Cockeysville Road Industrial Park.

THAMES STREET
From the 1400 block of Philpot Street east

The lively and picturesque waterfront heart of the trendy (and historic) Fells Point district. The London river was the obvious inspiration for this largely intact antique, dating from the eighteenth century.

Old-world Fells Point and Thames Street shine in a setting sun.

TIMONIUM ROAD
East and west from Exit 16, Interstate 83

A major east-west link that crosses the Baltimore-York freeway (Interstate 83), Timonium has variety; garden apartments, single family homes, a race track, boutique shopping, and open country. The name derives from Roman legend.

TINGES LANE
From the 3000 block of Old York Road north

Tiny Tinges Lane, almost buried behind the roaring traffic of 33rd and Greenmount Avenue, honors George W. Tinges, a wealthy nineteenth-century merchant. He had a fine estate from which he could see the hilltop mansions of the Sam Smith and Macdonald clans, but he moved out when somebody started one of the city's first subdivisions nearby in 1853. The Homestead section ran him out, and is now part of Waverly.

TIVOLI AVENUE
From the 1500 block of Roundhill Road south

This road runs from the edge of Clifton Park north to Northwood in the Loch Raven area. It is named for the estate of Enoch Pratt, the philanthropist who created the Baltimore library system. His many-windowed home has survived.

TOTTENHAM COURT ROAD
One block east of the 9100 block of Old Harford Road

Its name is copied from a famous London artery of Victorian days, and it leads a few blocks westward from Harford Road in suburban Carney.

TOWSON STREET (AND OTHERS)
From Latrobe Park and the 1500 block of East Fort Avenue north

Where do you start? It's a street in industrial Locust Point, an avenue in Country Club Park above Seminary Avenue, and in Towson town it is both a boulevard (in the county seat) and a court (in an apartment section near Charles Street). Nathan Towson was a War of 1812 hero, an artillerist who blew holes in the redcoat line at the Battle of Chippewa.

TRUXTUN STREET
One block north of East Madison Street near
900 Forrest Street

This street, apparent on city maps two generations ago, appears to have been swallowed up by enlargements to the state penitentiary on the margins of the midtown area. It's too bad, because Commodore Thomas Truxtun's ship, the U.S.S. *Constellation,* survives as the leading visual attraction of Baltimore's inner harbor. Truxtun took command of the ship in 1798 and blew the French ship, the *Insurgente,* out of the water in a famous fire fight. The street was named in 1822.

TUFTON AVENUE
From the 4100 block of Worthington Avenue
north

A superb country route through wealthy Worthington Valley, Tufton turns into a rush hour parade, handling cars commuting from Reisterstown subdivisions east to the populous, prosperous (14,000 jobs) Hunt Valley Industrial Park.

TYLER STREET (AND ROAD AND ALLEY)
From the 1500 block of Gorsuch Avenue south

John Tyler, tenth president of the U.S., suffers from bad publicity from historians because he was sympathetic to the South in the Civil War. But he was a firm president who did a good job. He was also a prolific daddy; he has middle-aged grandchildren living today. Tyler Street is a short lane in southern Waverly off Gorsuch Avenue. Tyler Road is in Fairway Park just east of Dundalk Community College. Tyler's Alley is in Old Town off President Street between Lombard and Pratt streets.

159

TYSON STREET
From the 200 block of West Read Street
northeast and south

He seemed quirky and far-out to his contemporaries, but the wealthy Quaker philanthropist Elisha Tyson was right in step with twentieth-century America in his call for racial equality. He spoke out fearlessly against slavery early in the nineteenth century, and helped to found Liberia. About 10,000 blacks attended his funeral in 1824. In the 1940s, Tyson Street's upper reaches on the west side of town were restored. Its modest row homes of the three-story Philadelphia type became an early model for colorful rehabs of decayed blocks.

Colorful renewal of tiny Tyson Street homes was sparked by a generation of sensitive rehabbing of historic properties.

UNION AVENUE
From the 3700 block of Roland Avenue
southwest

The heart of the Hampden area, with adjoining Hickory Avenue, these streets express almost everything that was said in brick, stone, and timber about modest housing in the mid- and late-nineteenth-century American milltown. The name probably derives from the neighborhood support of the Union in Civil War days. Though local rowdies once stoned a Yankee detachment for cutting off the cotton supply to local mills where they worked, Hampden and nearby Woodberry sent an entire militia unit off to fight for Abe and freedom in the 1860s.

UNIVERSITY PARKWAY
From the 3500 block of North Charles Street
east and west

A crosstown, almost wholly residential route (a major hospital intervenes) that links uppish Roland Park with old shoe Waverly. At one end is one of the city's only covered concrete bus stops; at the other is a roaringly successful farmer's market. In between, signs point to diversity like the Johns Hopkins Stadium and luxury condos with price tags as large as $1 million.

UPTON COURT (AND ROAD AND STREET)
Two blocks west of the 9300 block of Avondale Road

Upton is both a court and a road in the northeastern neighborhood of Thornwood Park, near Joppa and Harford roads near Carney. But it is also a short street on the near west side of town near Lafayette Square. The latter takes its name from an 1830s hilltop Greek Revival mansion (still standing) put up by Ed Ireland, a Baltimore man of means, 150 years ago. Now the whole area, thanks to a city rehab program, is called Upton. It's also

U

a subway stop. A second Upton Road exists in the St. John's Lane area of Howard County near U. S. 40 west, and a third road is off New Cut Road in upper Anne Arundel County. To finish the list, there's an Upton Avenue off Mapes Road in the same county near Fort Meade. The popularity of the Upton name is something of a mystery. Apparently, the classy overtones of the name are irresistable to developers.

Curious Lore

Central Avenue lies on top of the old Harford run, a stream carried down to the harbor under arched vaulting.

UTE COURT

From the 300 block of Ballard Avenue, Middle River, northeast

The Ute Indians used to help Kit Carson chase the Navahos. This apparent tribute to the great Colorado tribe, 1,500 miles east of their campfires, is in Ballard Gardens, a subdivision next door to the Village of Pawnee. Around the corner is Taos Court.

VENABLE AVENUE
From the 3300 block of Greenmount Avenue east

Dick Venable probably knew more about where things were in Baltimore, and what they were worth, than any man before or since. He was an unshakeable authority on real estate law. Using funds from a transit tax that had been cleverly restricted to park purposes, Venable enlarged existing parks and created new ones for the city. In 1916, a builder-friend named a new street Venable Avenue. It runs from the busy 33rd Street-Greenmount Avenue intersection in Waverly to the borders of Memorial Stadium.

VESTA AVENUE
Three blocks northeast of the 4400 block of Liberty Heights Avenue

Vesta Bloecher was ill. Her dad, a butcher turned real estate man, wanted to cheer her up. He named a street for her, one that stretches a short distance on the west side of the grounds of Forest Park High School.

VICKERS ROAD
From the 2600 block of North Hilton Street east

Banker George Vickers had wide interests—insect lore, astronomy, and bird shooting. His home was impressive enough for an estate title, "Mount Alto." Vickers Road is a dogleg in the Lake Ashburton area. Alto Road is further west in the Windsor Hills district.

VONDERHORST LANE
South from Sinclair Lane to the west side of Belair Road

A lane by this name was in evidence half a century ago, but it is not plotted on current directories. John H. Vonderhorst was a Hanoverian brewmaster who created the Eagle Brewery in the Belair Road area and operated it in the last four decades of the nineteenth century. He owned the world champion Baltimore Orioles of the 1890s.

163

WABASH AVENUE
From Butler Road south at the railroad bridge, Glyndon, and from the 4400 block of Patterson Avenue south

It's a double-header. One short avenue in the county suburb of Glyndon borders an old railroad line, and another borders the recently built subway in the northwest corridor. The former rail line took the faithful to camp meetings at the Methodist conference center at Emory Grove; the latter takes thousands to the Owings Mill Mall shopping center. There's a remnant of an older road alignment on the other side of the subway too, called Wabash Avenue East. The major Wabash Avenue divides the Pimlico and Arlington neighborhoods. The inspiration for the name is probably that Wabash (river) of Ohio and Indiana whose banks and sycamore trees were praised long ago in a turn-of-the-century song by Paul Dresser, "The Banks of the Wabash."

WAGNER STREET (AND LANE, ROAD, AND AVENUE)
From the 2300 block of Boston Street north

Wagner Street is a little Fells Point block off Boston Street. Frank Wagner was the genial canning king of the food trade, complete with mutton chop whiskers of the Chester Allen Arthur school, and a diamond stickpin below on his tie. His original plant was at the Fells Point location, but he moved to the other side of the harbor and built what amounted to a company town, with canning factory attached, at Curtis Creek. The other streets, not necessarily memorials to Frank, are a lane of Frog Mortar Creek out in eastern Baltimore County near Bowley's Quarters, a winding road in ritzy Ruxton and a short road in Glen Burnie, plus a waterfront affair fronting on Back River in Essex.

WALKER AVENUE
From the 6200 block of Loch Raven Boulevard
west

It's a crosstown route linking suburban Loch Raven Boulevard with York Road, honoring the late Henry M. Walker, wealthy owner of a well-known country estate, "Drumquehazel." Walker wanted to eliminate a buggy ride detour of two miles that he was forced to use to reach York Road from Hillen Road. Another Walker Avenue enters the campus of the University of Maryland, Baltimore County, off Wilkens Avenue, and still another runs off Route 175 in Fort Meade Heights. Howard County has a Walker Court off Frederick Road near the headwaters of the Patuxent River.

WALKER AVENUE
(PIKESVILLE)
From the unit block of Old Court Road west

Henry Walker's father, Patrick Henry Walker, had a great Pikesville farm, "Dumbarton," that was a model for Maryland agriculturists. Pat was the son of dry goods king Noah Walker, whose Baltimore Street store, with an illuminated statue of George Washington on its facade, was one of the tourist attractions of antebellum Baltimore. Pat Walker's avenue runs a few blocks off Old Court Road into the middle of Pikesville's busiest shopping area.

WALLIS AVENUE
From the 3500 block of Falstaff Road northwest

It's an upper Park Heights Avenue street that runs a few blocks through the extreme northwest corner of Baltimore. Severn T. Wallis, a giant of nineteenth-century legal history, was an aristocrat loyal to the North in the Civil War. But he never forgave the Union for locking up distinguished dissenters, himself included. He was one of the founders of the ancient Maryland Historical Society, established 1844.

WALTER AVENUE
From the 9400 block of Belair Road northwest

This one is a short street in Perry Hall, Baltimore County, not be confused with . . .

WALTHER AVENUE (AND BOULEVARD)
From the 4000 block of Harford Road northeast and from the 3300 block of East Joppa Road

Both of these are major crosstown routes. The boulevard leads south from the busy East Joppa Road area, with one interruption to Putty Hill Avenue near Parkville. Walther Avenue is an even bigger deal. It's a major arterial that takes off northeast from Harford Road in Herring Run Park, and connects with the Northern Parkway-Fleetwood Avenue interchange at Belair Road.

WARREN AVENUE
From the 900 block of Light Street east

A Federal Hill historic district attraction because of its village-like restoration of unique nineteenth-century row houses, Warren Avenue remembers Joseph Warren, the Massachusetts patriot who sent Paul Revere on his ride, then died in the Bunker Hill engagement. There's another Warren Avenue in Pikesville, and a third north of Baltimore-Washington International Airport, north of Fort Meade Road.

WASHINGTON BOULEVARD AND STREET
From the 200 block of South Paca Street southwest

At least fifteen metro area routes use the Washington name, possibly more. One historic route is Washington Boulevard, which starts virtually where the highrises end in center city, goes its way through a historic district and on into U.S. 1. The street, which is born at North

Hood Tires market their company symbol in an early billboard on billboard-infested Washington Boulevard (old U.S. 1), all paved and pretty in October 1919.

Avenue and goes straight as an arrow south to the Fells Point waterfront, is also historic. Washington Place is the name of a distinguished nineteenth-century promenade of buildings in the Mount Vernon district, adjoining the city's major monument to the first president.

WATER STREET
From the unit block of South Street east

A broken pathway threading through the highrise district and Maryland's most expensive land, Water Street is a relic of the Colonial era. Its eastern end has been revamped as an office and theme park region that has never quite clicked. It passes the city's handsome, neo-classic Customs House, famed for its gorgeous maritime murals.

WATKINS GLEN COURT
Five blocks east of York Road (10000 block) at Cranbrook Road

Woodstock Avenue northeast of Clifton Park is too old to commemorate the traditional name of the great 1970s rock and smoke fest, but if this street wasn't named after the festival's actual New York state site, then something is very strange. It's a short street off York Road in the Padonia section.

WATSON STREET
From the unit block of Central Avenue west

Watson Street runs three blocks, paralleling East Baltimore Street in the old Jonestown addition. It honors Col. William H. Watson, who died in the successful seige of Monterey in the Mexican War. His statue at North and Mount Royal avenues continues to bewilder all but knowledgeable history buffs.

WEBSTER STREET
South of the 700 block of East Fort Avenue

Lt. John Webster ran off the British barges attempting to land on the Fort McHenry peninsula in 1814. His South Baltimore street runs north and south near where it happened.

WELLS STREET
From the 1800 block of South Hanover Street east

It runs east and west near the south end of South Baltimore. Wells is one of two men (McComas is the other) believed to have shattered British resistance when they plugged General Robert Ross, the English commander of the assault on North Point in 1814.

WESLEY AVENUE
From the 3900 block of North Rogers Avenue
east and west

This street probably honors John Wesley, who gave birth
to Methodism. The road parallels Liberty Heights Avenue in the west side community of Howard Park.

WETHEREDSVILLE ROAD
From the 4500 block of Windsor Mill Road
northwest and southeast

John Wethered founded a cotton mill village in a west
Baltimore dale in the mid-nineteenth century. (Today the
area is known as Dickeyville). A souvenir of John and
his family remains in this long and loping route from
Forest Park Avenue to the middle of Gwynns Falls Park.
The Wethereds are supposed to have made some of their
money selling uniforms to the Confederate States Army.

WHISKEY BOTTOM ROAD
Northeast from Old Annapolis Road off State
Route 198

Both Anne Arundel and Howard counties share this
magnificently earthy street name. When bureaucrats
tried to change the name to something more dignified,
locals rose up in arms to preserve their street name and
its fine, honest colonial ring. The route is off Fort Meade
Road south of Annapolis Junction.

WHITEFORD AVENUE
From the 300 block of Winston Avenue north

It runs north and south a block or two east of the college
of Notre Dame of Maryland. Charlie Whiteford was a
Democratic politico of first-water talents. He ended his
career as clerk of the circuit court early in the twentieth
century.

169

WHITELOCK STREET
From the 2200 block of Mt. Royal Terrace west

The margins of the Reservoir Hill district have undergone restoration on the near northwest side of Baltimore, but the core of the pilot area remains troublesome and stagnant. Robert G. Whitelock was a mid-nineteenth-century American who married money and had a very large farm where his memorial street now runs.

WHITMORE AVENUE
From the 2500 block of Edmondson Avenue north

This street runs due south from the Walbrook area to West Franklin Street with an intermission for a few railroad tracks. The Webster Crowls, among founding families of the district, gave it the maiden name of a beloved friend.

WILKENS AVENUE
From the 1000 block of Rolling Road (Route 166) east

It's an inescapable and indispensable west side artery that feeds into the Baltimore beltway. It starts deep in southwest Baltimore and ends near a college campus in Baltimore County. A major hospital and the south edge of the city's largest cemetery (Loudon Park) are on its borders. The name derives from William Wilkens, founder of a "hair factory" that made hair pieces for the lavishly ornate coifs of Victorian women. Wilkens is famous for displaying the longest row housing in America, the 2600 block, with 104 dwellings stretched over 600 feet of "white steps."

WILSON STREET
From the 1600 block of Druid Hill Avenue east

A north Bolton Hill street that runs from John Street west through the Eutaw Place development and on to Pennsylvania Avenue. Wilson commemorates William Wilson, a master shipbuilder. He sponsored the great architect Robert Mills in construction of the First Baptist Church, a Greek Revival masterpiece that once stood at Sharp and Lombard streets.

WINANS WAY
From the 4600 block of Briarclift Road northeast and south

Tom Winans, the railroad pioneer hired by the Czar of Russia to engineer that country's railroads, joined the super-rich of the nineteenth century with the profits of the job. Winans Way, from Edmondson Avenue to the Franklintown Road intersection in Leakin Park, winds the way that a way should. It also is near "Crimea," the existing country estate that the Winans owned—it was paid for with Russian railroad profits.

WINCHESTER STREET
From the 1100 block of North Longwood Street east

This west Baltimore street does a stop and start routine east and west on the near west side of town. George Winchester was a sharp port attorney who was roughly handled in the city's Federalist riots of 1812.

WINDER STREET
From the 1900 block of South Charles Street east

It lies in the shadow of the Interstate 95 Fort McHenry tunnel approach. The Winders were prominent Maryland politicos and military men.

WINTON STREET
From the 3500 block of North Rogers Avenue northwest

Alex Winton was an auto pioneer of the 1890s. Winton Avenue, in the Ashburton area, was named in 1919 not for the man, but for the car that Winton produced in Cleveland.

WIRT AVENUE
From the 3300 block of Strathmore Avenue northwest and southeast

William Wirt was one of the greatest legal lights of the early republic. His street runs for a few blocks in the Cross Country Boulevard area in the northwestern corner of the city.

Curious Lore

Seven homes are split down the middle on the west side of East Boundary Avenue by the city-county line. "I eat in the city and sleep in the county," is a favorite quote of residents.

WOLFE STREET
From the 1700 block of East 25th Street south

An unchanging east side residential artery, Wolfe peels off from the Clifton Park area and drops southward for miles to end at or near the waterline in the north harbor. The honoree is General James Wolfe, who died at the Battle of Quebec when Baltimore was just a pup.

WOODALL STREET
From the 1000 block of East Fort Avenue northeast and southwest

This short Fort Avenue area street honors William E. Woodall, who rebuilt the U.S.S. *Wyoming* in Baltimore during the Civil War. The English immigrant's shipyard, Woodalls, near Federal Hill, flourished until 1929.

WRIGHT AVENUE
From the 4800 block of Erdman Avenue northeast

It's in the Armistead Gardens development put together to house World War II defense workers. There's an Orville and a Wilbur street, too, giving 100 percent coverage to the pioneering aviators.

Y

YORK ROAD
From the 500 block of East 42nd Street north to the Mason-Dixon Line

It is, of course, the ancient route to York, Pennsylvania, barbell and body building capital of the U.S.A., and one of two stars (Lancaster is the other) of the Amish and German farming heaven of Pennsylvania's eighteenth century. It's one of the eight great radials that shaped the city and put it on the map as a trade artery, even before railroading or international shipping. Of the eight, it features the fanciest residential real estate and the largest suburban town (Towson), and it is among the most historic, having been the path of a Confederate raid in the Civil War. North of Shawan, York is a largely preserved, nineteenth-century countryside. Below that are major shopping nodes and office parks, plus a notable small museum. The Fire Museum of Maryland, just north of Towson, is a roofed voyage back into horsedrawn days and the weekend of 1904, when the downtown burned way down to the ground.

Ulery's Govans Inn, a York Road resort in the horse and buggy days.

174

Neighborhoods

Baltimore, as any seasoned citizen will tell you, is not a city of streets like Paris, but a collection of small towns that grew up with a city—neighborhoods in a larger design. The identity and qualities differ. You can find everything from waterfront hideaways to barn and log cabin communities in high hill country. Well over 1,200 of these identifiable place names and neighborhoods are in the greater Baltimore area. Here is a sample of some of the best known, and some of the most representative.

ANNESLIE

An old country estate of towering Victorian lustre, still standing, gave its name to this attractive north end community east of York Road.

ARBUTUS

This woody name derives from creeping plants and evergreen trees. It's a southwestern neighborhood where they all go to church, and still remember Flag Day. Arbutus seems to have no recorded use as a U. S. place name, other than this.

175

The classic view of Baltimore's most beautiful sight. The Washington Monument and the terraced grandeur of Mount Vernon's gardens.

ARLINGTON

An encyclopedia of early-nineteenth-century modest housing, Arlington lies just south of Pimlico along close-in sections of Liberty Heights Avenue. Its Forest Park High School is famous for having incubated a generation of kids who went on to fame in the Hollywood-New York entertainment world. No less than twenty-six American places claim this name, including the nation's most famous cemetery.

BEVERLY HILLS

Yes, Maryland (and Virginia), there is a Beverly Hills East, bordered by Harford Road and Walther Avenue. It was started in 1926, and may be almost as old as the homes of the stars in Los Angeles.

176

BOLTON HILL

(see Mount Royal)

BROOKLANDVILLE

A once-remote, now busy crossroads due north of town. It boasts a boutique shopping center, deluxe private schools, and housing that can easily be afforded by mortgage bankers, surgeons, and major league sports stars.

BROOKLYN

One of the city's oldest middle class suburbs. Founded long before the Civil War, it is situated due south of center city and across the waters of the middle branch of the Patapsco River. Parts of it have a distinctly nineteenth-century air. It's one of seven U. S. Brooklyns, including the one that used to have the Dodgers.

CANTON

Named for the Chinese port by shippers nearly two centuries ago, Canton, for 150 years, housed the core of the city's metal and oil manufacturing. Today, oddly, it is emerging from the rust belt to become a swank marina community.

CEDONIA

A far east-side community, just inside the city line west of Gardenville, much of Cedonia is recently built. Belair Road and Frankford and Radecke avenues define the locale generally.

CHARLES VILLAGE

From 20th Street north to the Hopkins University campus, Charles Village (formerly Peabody Heights), features a variety of housing choices for income groups. Couples and singles are recycling 1900-era buildings near Johns Hopkins University.

Vast mansions were built in the Mount Vernon and midtown sections of Baltimore in the late Victorian period. This was the St. Paul Street home of the first president of Goucher College, famed women's, now coed, institute of higher education. Stanford White's firm designed the building.

CHERRY HILL

A general hospital, a waterfront park, and three major schools are amenities in this 1950s urban planned community. It overlooks the widest part of the Patapsco's middle branch.

CLIFTON PARK

One of the city's largest parks lies in the midst of this early-twentieth-century neighborhood between Belair and Harford roads. The star of the show is "Clifton," the towering Italian villa and onetime summer home of Johns Hopkins. The city's most historic Jewish cemetery is also included in the area.

COCKEYSVILLE

Once just a quarry or two and a hay barn haven, Cockeysville has emerged as a dense apartment and single family home community since World War II. Hunt Valley Industrial Park, a service industry heaven between York Road and Interstate 83, is its proudest success story.

DICKEYVILLE

A picture perfect nineteenth-century village restoration, Dickeyville pioneered fixing up the city's innumerable old mill towns. Buried in greenery and all but invisible, it lies west of Windsor Hills and the last stretches of Gwynns Falls Park.

DUNDALK

One of the city's earliest planned suburban communities, Dundalk has been vastly enlarged by middle class row housing stretching for miles to the southeast. It trails off into miles of quiet shoreline off Bear Creek. The name was inspired by an Irish seaside district north of Dublin.

EASTPOINT

A small but busily strategic community serving as sort of a gateway to the vast Dundalk-Sparrows Point residential and industrial region. The star of the show is Eastpoint Mall, a spectacular 1950s retailing success.

179

The first great eastside shopping breakthrough in suburban marketing and convenience, Eastpoint Mall, with a full lot on a 1950s weekend. Eastern Avenue is on the left, North Point Boulevard on the right.

Today it has shed upscale department stores for discount retailing and family oriented retailing giants like Sears.

EDGEMERE

It's a major community on the long North Point Road route to Sparrows Point. Two waterfronts and a huge park frontage make it unusual.

180

ELKRIDGE

A historic, hilly west-side community that was both a Civil War defense point and a turn-of-the-century resort of the streetcar suburb type. The legal profession gathered here in the good old days, giving the name "Lawyer's Hill" to one section of Elkridge. The valley below is famous as a distillery center.

ELLICOTT CITY

Named for a famous founding family of mill owners and surveyors, this nineteenth-century town is the most picturesque and romantic in the metro area. It tumbles down a Howard County hill. Heavily damaged in a 1972 flood, it staged a comeback as a regional antique haunt.

ESSEX

A further eastern twin of Dundalk, the community has recently restyled its downtown and restored historic attractions like Balleston Manor. The name was apparently inspired by Essex, a London metro-area county with a larger population than all of Baltimore.

FEDERAL HILL

A remarkable success story in urban rehabbing, this section's once-deteriorated nineteenth-century relics have been intensively redone. Today it is a first choice harbor location. The view from historic Federal Hill Park gives Baltimore's miniature version of the lower Manhattan skyline.

FELLS POINT

A shade older than the oldest Baltimore sections, Fells Point staged a comeback a generation ago. It now blends restored housing and a few nationally important samples of eighteenth-century merchant housing, with a plethora of restaurants and night spots.

The Civil War headquarters of General Ben Butler on Federal Hill, near the present site of Warren Avenue.

Union troops aim their guns at the streets of downtown Baltimore from the ramparts of Federal Hill (photo from about 1862).

182

Duryea's dashing New York militia encamped on Federal Hill about 1862. They would be butchered at Gettysburg.

FERNDALE

A large middle-income suburb south of the Beltway near Glen Burnie that surrounds a school complex. Main access roads include Maryland 3 and old Annapolis Road. Seven American communities bear this name, including a biggie near Detroit.

FOREST PARK

Featuring some of the finest suburban housing of the 1920s and 1930s, this close-in, racially integrated neighborhood appeals to large families and professionals who shun the ordeals of long distance commuting.

FULLERTON

A community off the outer Belair Road, Fullerton fronts on one of the largest areas of undeveloped land close to the city. Housing borders the Fullerton reservoir site. Though it sounds original, there are plenty of U. S. Fullertons, the biggest in California, the smallest a North Dakota village.

GARDENVILLE

A pleasant and densely domestic neighborhood on the northeast side of town on both sides of endless Belair Road. It emerged from farming in the late nineteenth century, and is one of the last spots in the urban region where super-handymen once built their own houses and then moved in. Buffalo, New York, has a twin in name.

GLEN BURNIE

Largest and most complex of the city's south suburbs, Glen Burnie is traditionally thought of as a suburban blah. Actually, it outperforms many other metro areas in wealth of suburban services. Its downtown is being restyled, and its south edge features unrivaled reception of electronic media in the six million-population Baltimore-Washington-Annapolis areas. Glen Burnies, a tribute to Scotland, also exist in Maine and North Dakota.

GLENMONT

A single family and apartment community just over the city line between the Country Club of Maryland and Loch Raven Boulevard.

GLYNDON

With its historic Emory Grove Methodist camp ground and a wealth of porchy Victorian architecture, Glyndon is a popular destination for outer suburban affluents. Far off, and no doubt far different, is Glyndon, Minnesota, near the North Dakota line.

GOVANS

Probably Scotch in inspiration (a suburb of Glasgow), Govans was once a town, and today is an important home and shopping community in the middle stretches of York Road. A new and elaborate shopping center there has been a rousing success, surprising the Maryland retailing community.

GUILFORD

The ultimate in "conventional" mansion-sized living of the forty-foot living room type, Guilford was created in the F. Scott Fitzgerald era in the city's priciest residential region, north of University Parkway. The name derives from the estate of a wealthy sportsman of the early nineteenth century. "Guilford" contained more than fifty rooms.

HALETHORPE

An apparently original name that is not repeated in U. S. atlases, Halethorpe is a virtual twin of middle-income Arbutus, off the southwestern margins of town and U.S. 1. It is defined by Southwestern Boulevard and the main line of the B&O railroad.

HAMILTON

This quiet, stable specimen of middle America, eastern style, lies between Harford and Belair roads—a veritable museum of bungalow, Dutch colonial and shingle style architecture of the early twentieth century. Garden plots abound in Hamilton, and the Christmas light shows border on the unbelievable. A ghost town in Nevada and a big town in Ontario have the Hamilton name, plus about twenty-six U.S. counties and towns.

HAMPDEN

Stone buildings and frame homes abound here, along with some of the city's housing bargains, in an old mill town setting overlooking the Jones Falls Valley. Front porch lifestyles and 100 percent Americanism are featured. Its main stem, 36th Street, once the model of a small town downtown within a big city, is staging a comeback.

The Hampden-Woodberry mill valley with views of the Jones Falls and Falls Road, a stereo from around 1870.

HAMPTON

A region whose stars are nationally-known Goucher College, plus the Hampton Mansion Historic Monument (the largest Colonial-era house in Maryland), Hampton also has deluxe housing south of Seminary Avenue and north of the Beltway.

HIGHLANDTOWN

Rock solid, hilly Highlandtown on the east side has lost its industrial lustre as the brewing capital of Maryland, but it doesn't seem to care about that. Its yellow brick, incredibly affordable row homes, with their stained glass windows and marble steps, are an indestructable image of Baltimore's city tradition. Some of the grand-children of original residents are moving back.

HOMELAND

Named for a famed Greek revival country estate, it has been the happy home of corporate execs and families who want luxury on a convenient city site. The brick and stone styling of 1920s and 1930s origin and the area's landscaping are a breathtaking trip back into a kinder and gentler America. The azalea plantings are famous.

186

IDLEWYLDE

A small residential area between Regester Avenue and the city line west of the Anneslie area. The name and its fanciful spelling are almost a description of mid-century residential dreams.

INVERNESS

This small residential community within the Dundalk area has three waterfront exposures; Chink Creek, Lynch Cove, and the main arm of Bear Creek. Across the water is the Sparrows Point Country Club. The name is of Scotch origin.

IRVINGTON

A major outer west-side area with modest and affordable housing, north of Frederick Avenue (Route 144) and near the city line. It awaits, and probably will receive, discovery by the yuppie generation. There are six U. S. towns and villages of this name, most all, including this one, probably a tribute to author Washington Irving.

Three street urchins pose on the cobblestones in a South Baltimore slum that Charles Dickens might have described 100 years earlier. Houses like these are being rapidly restored, and now command prices of five and six figures.

LANSDOWNE

A major residential and industrial park district just over the southwestern city line, Lansdowne is one of those areas that rarely changes in basic qualities over the years. It is almost completely ringed by the Baltimore Parkway, the Beltway, U.S. 1, and Patapsco Avenue. Within this pentagon-shaped area are two lakes, five schools, and a good many happy homeowners. It is also a borough in Delaware, a village in Ontario, and an India mountain town named for a British lord.

LINTHICUM

A sturdy, long-established residential area south of the city. It is northeast of Baltimore-Washington International Airport, and is bisected by Hammond's Ferry Road. Linthicum is made up of about ten north-Anne Arundel County subdivisions west of Ferndale. Commuter rail lines, Fort Meade Road and the Baltimore-Washington Parkway crisscross the area.

LOCH RAVEN

The generic name for a brace of recently built suburban residential clusters east of Towson off the boulevard of the same name. There's another Loch Raven area, too, further north near the Loch Raven reservoir.

LOCHEARN

Quality builders in the 1920s and 1930s, and again in the 1950s, completed this leafy, attractive place. It has small and medium sized residential buildings, varied in architecture. It is on a site off Liberty Heights Avenue just over the city line.

188

LUTHERVILLE

Educational hopefuls founded a college (since extinct) here in the 1850s. Residents piled in to escape Baltimore's heat, and they still do, though Lutherville is now very much for year-round living. Its important Victorian buildings are well preserved. There's another Lutherville in Meriwether County, Georgia.

MARGATE

One of Anne Arundel County's numerous water oriented, clubby home communities east of Glen Burnie. Its counterpart in England is a sort of Ocean City, the state's No. 1 sea and sand resort.

MAYFIELD

An ancient crossroads in Howard County where the old National Pike (U. S. 40) crosses Triadelphia Road, Mayfield leads southward to such open country home sections as Evergreen Valley estates and Woodmark.

MIDDLE RIVER

A blue collar haven that blossomed in World War II as an aviation center, this area has since diversified to embrace new economic conditions. A permanent plus is access to Bay boating, east-side shopping and industrial park employment.

MONDAWMIN

Originally an estate held by members of the Alex. Brown investment banking family, today it is mostly early-twentieth-century homes, a shopping mall with subway stop, and the place where important arteries, Reisterstown Road and Liberty Heights Avenue, begin.

MONTEBELLO HEIGHTS

The original Montebello was the superb Federal-era home of Sam Smith, the great War of 1812 hero. This community is some distance to the northeast of the home site, however. Areas like this, of the early twentieth century, show unequalled craftsmanship.

MORNINGSIDE HEIGHTS

An Owings Mills community notable for having pioneered the recreation, leisure living, or club lifestyle in the Baltimore apartment market.

MORRELL PARK

A long-established home community off outer Washington Boulevard. A humorous feature of its street titling is Maudlin Avenue.

Charles Carroll's fine colonial mansion is near Morrell Park.

MOUNT CLARE

One of the most important sites in U.S. railroading history, Mount Clare now features the magnificent B&O Railroad Museum, one of the world's finest industrial displays. The nearby Poppleton restoration district is giving a new direction to once-dreary southwest Baltimore.

MOUNT ROYAL

The chunk of old Baltimore from the state office center off Howard Street north to Druid Hill Park, Mount Royal includes the sometimes showy nineteenth-century home restorations of Bolton Hill and Reservoir Hill. The name, which dates back to 1720, appears to be fading out in contemporary usage in favor of the smarter "hills."

The hub of Mount Royal area travel, the Mount Royal station of the Pennsylvania Railroad. Wagons and street cars serviced the train station area from North Charles Street.

MOUNT VERNON

Maryland's most dazzling exhibit of nineteenth-century traditional homes, with amenities attached; libraries, concert halls, and museums. Late-nineteenth-century Mrs. Astorbilt types had town houses and Rembrandts here.

MOUNT WASHINGTON

One of the city's oldest and prettiest street railway suburbs, nearing its 150th year. A boutique and gourmet shopping center is part of the package.

MURRAY HILL

Enoch Pratt, the great library philanthropist, used to own this north Baltimore hillside tract off upper Charles Street. Today its large and swanky homes shelter executives and professionals and their families.

NOB HILL

A mature suburb built in open farm country off Route 140, Nob Hill was once far on the outer ring of development. It's now closest to the residential boom that is spreading northwest to Westminster, the Carroll County capital.

NORMANDY

This is the center of a cluster of home communities on both sides of historic Route 40 West (the National Road) dating back to Jefferson's day. Its shopping center was one of the earliest in the rapid 1960s development of Howard County.

NORTH POINT

Vast and sprawling North Point is two things; the largest developed peninsula of the metro area or, more properly, a secluded Back River waterfront home section northeast of the Patapsco freeway (U.S. 695). The former has dozens of small subdivisions; the latter has streets named in honor of Jean, Stefan, Greg and Les—all members of the Gunzelman family who operate Briarwood, a family-owned trailer park where the names of the streets appear.

O'DONNELL HEIGHTS

Built in the World War II era as defense housing, and government managed, O'Donnell Heights lapsed into a problem area. Now it's been refurbished. The Heights are a commanding part of the city's natural nineteenth-century defense system.

OELLA

One of the area's most remarkable restorations is this tumbling hillside of a town on the Patapsco River. Once derelict and downtrodden, it is now in a comeback stage. It's just opposite the Ellicott City restoration, the antique capital of the city's west side.

OLD MILL

A big slice of Anne Arundel County suburbia, Old Mill features cute and "colonial" middle class building styles in the Quarterfield Road and Route 100 areas.

OVERLEA

One of Baltimore's numerous middle-America haunts, Overlea was built early in the century south of Double Rock Park, and bridged by Belair Road and Taylor Avenue. It has an air of privacy, coupled with exceptional Beltway access.

Thanks, but I'm Buying a Condo

Some street names can make you downright uneasy. Witness Blister Street, Croissant Road, Cuckold Point Road, Deviation Road, Feign Court, Blobs Road, and Bump Court. And some ask questions, like Annawon Court (but what did she win?), an Anne Arundel County puzzler. Deviation Road is perfectly straight, while Curving Lane in Ruxton appears to be so named because it does.

OWINGS MILLS

At the end of the present subway line, this region has blossomed as the No. 1 yuppie residential area for downtown workers. A glittery mall is the centerpiece, plus office parks and "clean" industry.

PARADISE

It's a strip of pre-World War II America that lies along Frederick Road en route to Catonsville. If you close your eyes, you can hear the trolleys that used to clang, clang, clang east and west in the days of straw hats and bustles.

PARKVILLE

The world's third largest American Legion post is a major attraction in patriotic Parkville's never-changing landscape. It's a mom and pop place, rich in values. Sister name-places are a village in York County, Pennsylvania, and a river town near Kansas City, Missouri.

PERRY HALL

It used to be the place you drove to on a day's outing to shop for fruit and vegetables. Today it is a stable community with half a dozen developments named in its honor along Belair Road as it hurries northeast toward the Gunpowder River.

Intermittent snows are the bane of city drivers. Here is a cooperative effort to get things going around 1960, at the height of the gas guzzling, fin-tailed era of auto design.

PIKESVILLE

The gourmet capital of the city. With delis, bakeries and super supermarkets, Pikesville caters to the well-to-do shoppers of Reisterstown Road, who buy both dough-nuts and diamonds. The area features deluxe apart-ments, and a historic armory that served for decades as the home for Maryland's Confederate veterans.

PIMLICO

Some of the finest, and worst, of city housing surrounds the famous race track, second stop on the Triple Crown circuit. Just to the east is the nationally important Sinai Hospital Center.

POPLAR HILL

Traditional mansions nestled in the moneyed Lake Av-enue district, Poplar Hill is the sort of place where every other house has a tennis court.

POT SPRING

Eastern Timonium's most deluxe residential neighbor-hood, Pot Spring's winding, pretty roads include luxury residences like ten-room ranch houses and the sort of stone-faced "colonials" they don't build much anymore.

PUTTY HILL

Like Perry Hall, its neighbor further north, the Putty Hill area along U.S. 1 is family-oriented. A club cellar sort of place, it has surprisingly rural accents here and there in the midst of neat lawns, fencing, and the putter of power mowers.

RAMBLEWOOD

A Belvedere Avenue district in the northeast end of town, Ramblewood earned fame beyond its size as a "hot" residential area, with appreciations that drew applause. It remains well kept and attractive.

RANDALLSTOWN

A onetime village far to the west in Baltimore County, Randallstown was the sort of place that used to run out of water every now and then because of altitude. Randallstown today is a complex blend of housing and shopping for the young, many of whom commute to center city or points in between by way of the subway.

RAVENHURST

A quite deluxe, but representative north Baltimore county haven along the Dulaney Valley branch, with large, expensive housing. It is named after a fantastic Gothic-style summer mansion that burned, home of Gen. I. Ridgeway Trimble, C.S.A., one of the South's most feared commanders.

REISTERSTOWN

A northwest county hub, this community's traffic gridlock (and part of its customers) moved elsewhere with the completion of the Northwestern Freeway (Interstate 795). It's an antique hub, with many nineteenth-century buildings surviving.

Harrison Rider, prominent and wealthy. His Methodist friends purified their neighborhood in the prohibition days by naming the area after him, dodging a liquor-soaked brand name.

RIDERWOOD

An old station stop for the railroad, Riderwood became a commuter suburb back in the 1880s for staid, wealthy people. A big selling point for the estates and summer places was that from the hills you could see both the county courthouse and the local insane asylum.

RIDGEWAY

The first in a series of attractive home communities west of old Catonsville. It's a popular name, with two Ridgeways in Iowa, and one each in Missouri, Ohio, South Carolina and Virginia.

ROCKLAND

An unusual early-nineteenth-century mill village, restored with loving care in the Falls Road corridor. Dorothy Lamour once ran a cosmetic factory here.

RODGERS FORGE

The happy, row house home of everybody young who was expecting a first or second kid in the mid-century years. Since then, these homes have commanded ten or twelve times their original purchase price. End rows are regarded as especially choice.

ROLAND PARK

One of the earliest planned communities of the late-Victorian era, this section has offered quiet shelter to as many as five generations of the well-heeled. Its folkways are immortalized in the novels of the Pulitzer prize-winning author Anne Tyler.

ROSEDALE

It's a slice of the older America, just beyond the county line in the hilly section of the Philadelphia Road (Route 7). It is one of the few city areas with numbered streets; it is also subject to occasional high winds.

A street parade of taxicabs advertising the "lowest fares in town" on a spring morning in Roland Park, 1921.

ROSSVILLE

A wide-open space that is mostly industrial parkland and community college. Rossville features one fascination in nomenclature—a Yellow Brick Road leading off Rossville Boulevard to the northeast.

RUXTON

A north county residential area with homes dating back to late Victorian. These homes appeal to old or new homeowners who want a five-acre lot, six bedrooms, and a steep six-figure tag. Ruxton is all but invisible from important arteries that skirt it.

SAGAMORE FOREST

One of several secluded new subdivisions that overlooks the old Vanderbilt horse farm in the gorgeous Worthington Valley. The name origin is obscure, but Sagamore is a village in Massachusetts, a place in Pennsylvania, and an older suburb of Cleveland.

SCOTT'S LEVEL

An old county place name is borne by this housing area adjoining the Old Court Middle School near the city's next-to-last subway stop.

SEVERN

Virtually surrounded by open land, the Severn communities near Fort Meade center around Lake Marion in Anne Arundel County. The name, of Welsh origin, is duplicated in Ontario and Australia.

SHAWAN

A small north Baltimore County crossroads that features a boutique shopping center, a vineyard, and giant mansion-estates inhabited by wealthy bluebloods and corporate moguls.

SOLLER'S POINT

Dundalk Avenue and the Key Bridge approaches (Main Street) define this waterbound community, along with Peachorchard and Clement coves. It is one of the more accessible "shore" residential haunts available with a short ride from the city's east side.

SPARROW'S POINT

A once-mighty Bethlehem Steel plant, reduced to about one-fourth of its original employment force, is the main industrial feature of this huge peninsula. It was created, complete with a planned company town and golf course, early in the twentieth century.

SPRINGDALE

A deluxe housing community with active growth in the 1960s and 1970s, it fronts on the never-to-be-developed Loch Raven watershed.

STONELEIGH

A sort of "younger brother" of stylish Homeland, Stoneleigh lies on the opposite side of York Road. It's also a village in Shakespeare's Avon country in England.

STEVENSON

A smart north county address with a small, very foxy shopping center, and a professional office hub. Area housing is rarely sold. Stevenson is also a town in Alabama and a city in southwestern Washington state.

SUDBROOK PARK

A very early planned home community on the north-western segment of the urban area. Winding streets and the homes both reflect the touch of Frederick Law Olmsted, Jr., of the family that created Central Park, Manhattan.

TEN HILLS

A mid-century, far west end development with fine specimens of 1930s-quality construction, built when labor was $2 an hour and sand was free. Uplands Park provides a green belt in the area.

TIMONIUM

The generic name for the dense mixture of state fairgrounds, shopping centers, and apartment and single family housing that has grown up in the last half of the twentieth century, north of the city and the Beltway.

TOWSON

Baltimore county's largely unplanned and all-important political capital, now the hive of major national brokerage firms and legal big shots. A revitalized mall and senior citizen housing are new notes here. One old one is a fine vintage courthouse of pre-Civil War era stonework. Joppa Road's spectacular hillside housing west of downtown recalls Berkeley, California. Another peculiar feature is a stone-walled housing project in the middle of the downtown, said to never have had a vacancy in half a century.

Nathan Towson's guns mattered in the 1812 war; his name adorns Baltimore's largest suburban node.

VICTORY VILLA

World War II housing in the Martin Boulevard area. Now the granddaddy of dozens of newer streets in sections stretching northeast into open country.

VILLAGE OF CROSS KEYS

The Rouse Company, international developers, created this still-stylish village in the Jones Falls Valley during the 1960s. It served as a study for their huge, 14,000-acre Baltimore-Washington city, Columbia. Its shopping mall is one of the smartest in central Maryland, and the residential mix includes town houses, condos, and apartments.

VIOLETVILLE

It's in the southwestern city near St. Agnes Hospital, a liveable middle-income area close to town between Interstate 95 and Southwestern Boulevard. The local fire department is a classic mainstay of area parades.

WALBROOK

They used to call it the "junction," because this is where the major street railways turned around. Doctors and other professionals built it up in the 1880s; architecturally it is a goldmine of the "Queen Anne" style. A partial comeback from 1950s deterioration is underway.

WALTHERSON

One of the innumerable solid subdivisons of homes that dot both sides of Harford Road, Waltherson is one of those with the closest access to center city.

WAVERLY

A hub of near-north-side living around 33rd Street and Greenmount Avenue, Waverly has dense neighborhood development, dating back into the early nineteenth century in some cases. Its Memorial Stadium site may be redeveloped, which could alter the realty picture.

WESTPORT

A heavily industrial section off the upper stretches of Russell Street, due south of center city, with access to the spaghetti of interstate routes feeding the harbor area.

WHITE MARSH

An east side commercial success story after it cornered a major shopping center developer in the 1980s. White Marsh has revived the allure of the east sections of old Philadelphia Road and U.S. 40, overshadowed for a while by Interstate 95.

WILTONDALE

One of the numerous pleasant and rather pricey suburbs that line both sides of the upper York Road south of Towson. The handsome Country Club of Maryland is the main local amenity.

Curious Lore

Famed Waterloo Row (the 600 block of Calvert Street), designed by Robert Mills and destroyed in 1968, *was not original*. The architect practiced by doing a Philadelphia version of the urban row houses at Ninth and Locust streets in 1809.

WOODLAWN

The bedroom community for the giant U.S. Social Security Administration headquarters, Woodlawn has a dense mix of apartment and single family living, some of it dating from the early twentieth century.

WOODMOOR

This quality subdivision south of Liberty Road in the city's west end was developed in a contour pattern of circling streets, back in the early part of the century, when suburban planning embraced art.

Index